The
LOVERS'
TAROT

The LOVERS' TAROT

Robert Mueller, Ph.D., and
Signe E. Echols, M.S., with Sandra A. Thomson

AVON BOOKS ◆ NEW YORK

THE LOVERS' TAROT is an original publication of Avon Books. This work has never before appeared in book form.

Illustrations from the *Rider-Waite Tarot* deck reproduced by permission of U.S. Games Systems, Inc., Stamford, CT 06902 USA. Copyright © 1971 by U.S. Games Systems, Inc. Further reproduction prohibited.

AVON BOOKS
A division of
The Hearst Corporation
1350 Avenue of the Americas
New York, New York 10019

Copyright © 1993 by Robert E. Mueller, Ph.D., Signe E. Echols and Sandra Thomson
Interior design by Robin Arzt
Published by arrangement with the authors
Library of Congress Catalog Card Number: 92-24147
ISBN: 0-380-76886-0

Library of Congress Cataloging in Publication Data:
Mueller, Robert E. (Robert Eugene).
   The lovers' tarot / Robert Mueller and Signe E. Echols, with Sandra A. Thomson.
      p. cm.
Includes bibliographical references and index.
1. Tarot. 2. Interpersonal relations—Miscellanea. 3. Love—Miscellanea. I. Echols, Signe E. II. Thomson, Sandra A. III. Title.
BF1879.T2M84   1993   92-24147
133.3'2424—dc20   CIP

First Avon Books Trade Printing: February 1993

AVON TRADEMARK REG. U.S. PAT. OFF. AND IN OTHER COUNTRIES, MARCA REGISTRADA, HECHO EN U.S.A.

Printed in the U.S.A.

OPM   10 9 8 7 6 5 4 3 2 1

We dedicate this book:

To the loving memory of Signe's parents,
Ellen Elizabeth Hoyer Newbury
and Charles Benjamin Newbury Jr.

And to the memory of Robert's father, Eugene G. Mueller.
You made me practice writing my name
because someday I would need to put it on something.
Well, Dad, here it is.

And to Carol, of course.

ACKNOWLEDGMENTS

Signe E. Echols wants to express thanks and appreciation to:

Dr. Stephan Hoeller, who introduced me to Tarot and inspired further study and practice. His lectures on Gnosticism and Jungian psychology added to my understanding of symbology.

The Reverend Trudy Jarno, pastor of the Church of Inner Light, for her continuing inspiration and encouragement and for providing an opportunity for me to develop my psychic potential.

The other ministers on the church's staff and the members of the congregation for their appreciation and encouragement.

Fred Hansen, president of the United Sensitives of America, for his efforts to establish professional status and a platform for psychic readings, and for enabling me to expand my abilities.

Peter Balin, author of *The Flight of Feathered Serpent,* for his unique approach to the story of the cards.

My brother, Charles B. Newbury, for his personal encouragement.

Robert E. Mueller expresses his thanks and appreciation to:

My mother, Evelyn Mueller, who has always believed in me. I could not have done without her help. She ran countless errands without complaint, which allowed me the time to read, write, and struggle to produce this book.

Simone, my first psychic teacher. After I realized the unconscious communicated through symbols, she directed me to Jerry Terranova's Tarot classes. His wise and gentle ways started me on the Tarot path. His classes in numerology proved an invaluable tool in my life.

The following Tarot teachers who expanded my insight and depth of understanding, allowing me to see in totally new ways: Laura Jennings, James Wanless, Eileen Connolly, and Stephan Hoeller. They each have contributed to give me direction and wisdom in my personal life.

To Bunny Rosenzweig, who, with a turn of the phrase, tossed us the Tarot for Two tidbit and completely won us over.

All three authors express their indebtedness to:

Roger Weir, whose lectures on ancient wisdom teachings at the Philosophical Research Society and the Whirling Rainbow Institute gave us an appreciation of the values that spiritual development can bring to a relationship. His philosophical interpretation of the occult path created and inspired fresh and novel thought patterns.

Georgia Lambert R. for her ongoing classes on the nature of the soul and on meditation techniques, which provided an inner focus for selecting many of the meanings and symbology in this book and which sharpened that focus by teaching us to clear away nonessentials.

Paul Foster Case's Builders of the Adytum for their in-depth Tarot teachings.

Anita Weld for her thoughtful editorial counsel during early drafts of the book.

Our agent, Bob Silverstein, whose vision was instrumental in shaping this book, and our editor at Avon, Chris Miller, who kept us literate and user-friendly.

Our students who worked through earlier sections of this manuscript, and our clients for whom we have done Tarot for Two readings. Too often their feedback forced us to reformulate our ideas, and occasionally allowed us to bask in the satisfaction of those that worked.

CONTENTS

Part 3: Tarot Tips

Part 4: Tarot for Two

Part 5: Tarotscapes

FOREWORD

Relationships, which nurture the unfolding of ourselves and others, are perhaps the greatest path for personal growth. Seeing ourselves in relation to others, we co-create and grow.

Every relationship is a two-way mirror. Tarotscapes use cards and their symbols to construct that mirror. The Tarot for Two process transforms the symbolic system of the Tarot into an interactive dialogue. Through this exchange we clarify our uniqueness, our strengths, and our weaknesses.

Tarot is used here as a way of communicating, which is the heart and soul of any relationship. During this conversation, as it is structured in *The Lovers' Tarot,* we see how we project our own self-image onto others. We see ourselves through how we see one another. The wonderful aspect of this book is that we get to know our many different selves and create a healthy self-relationship, which is the basis for any successful relationship with others.

All relationships are fluid and evolving. Dialoguing with a partner through the Tarot is a way of staying in balance with those changes. Relationships need maintenance and guidance as well. *The Lovers' Tarot* gives a step-by-step process for examining and directing relationships. Tarot for Two is the navigation chart for mapping the course of any partnership.

To stay current with the ebb and flow of a relationship means being able to see the interaction from different viewpoints. Like a crystal, the Tarot exposes, through its facets, the many possibilities of a relationship. The Tarot for Two approach offers ways to highlight those facets, to polish them, to smooth out the rough spots.

Albert Einstein said, "The formulation of the question is far more important than the answer." How we look at a relationship and the kinds of questions we ask of it are of critical importance.

The genius of this book is its presentation for formulating those questions. *The Lovers' Tarot* pays considerable attention to this often neglected aspect.

The value of assessing relationships through the Tarot lies in the stimulating ideas and perspectives from the inner self which the picture symbols spark. An information system that accesses intuition, Tarot draws upon honesty, relevance, and creativity. Relationships cannot exist without such truth and renewal. Tarot is a wondrous way to keep relationships alive and healthy, and *The Lovers' Tarot* offers a framework that is flexible and open enough for emerging issues to be addressed.

James Wanless, Ph.D.
Author of *Voyager Tarot*
Carmel, California

INTRODUCTION:
VIEWING YOURSELF AND OTHERS FROM THE TAROT PERSPECTIVE

There is no better way to enter into the process of self-understanding than through the Tarot, and few more accessible ways to enter into communication with another than through a Tarot reading.

While you may bring a personal bias or special interest to the reading, the end purpose of any Tarot reading is that growth takes place, that you move out of a problem area with clarity. *The Lovers' Tarot* teaches you one way to do that.

Like all professions, the learning of the Tarot requires long preparation. I am gratified to see excellent study courses and workbooks finding their way into the market. The works of James Wanless and Mary K. Greer, all excellent, are now joined by this one on the Tarot for Two, which I have been asked to introduce.

I have known Signe Echols, one of the authors of *The Lovers' Tarot*, for many years. She has worked with diligence to perfect her craft. She has studied and practiced not only the discipline of the Tarot, but other, related disciplines as well. She brings to this book valuable practical experience.

My own entrance into the world of Tarot occurred more than fifteen years ago with the Xultun Tarot, a deck I painted and produced utilizing Mayan Indian imagery. I am told that the Mayan deck opened the gates for a flood of new and interesting systems that have since become available.

As a result, interest in the Tarot has multiplied and people are beginning to understand its implications. Tarot is not facile, so people are willingly entering into a discipline that requires time and the gaining of depth beyond the fads of our day.

Tarot is a system of metaphor, so individuals are beginning to see their lives not just as a linear journey, but more as a hero's adventure. This leads to an open view of experience and the need for a suitable mythologem from which to piece together life's varied experiences. The Tarot is ideally suited to these tasks.

If we are to escape the traps of blame, guilt, and self-incrimination so characteristic of past views of the world—if we are to understand that our way of seeing the world is exactly that, only a view—then the Tarot offers a window through which not only *that* view is possible, but more than one view can be accessed.

A broader perspective allows us to understand that we are larger, and—if it is a true experience, not just an ego inflation—shows us that others also are larger than we at first thought. A view is just that, merely a view—ever changing as we ourselves change and grow. Never static, too often resembling glimpses from the window of a speeding train, the expanded view is, of course, the depth of our life as we pursue its progression from beginning through middle to end.

Since most of life takes place in that middle range, it has few unalterable truths and is *all* relationship. Any Tarot book is useful only if it leads us to discover our own view, which can never be in isolation. The "truth of being" is always in relationship, as the Tarot for Two layout so aptly shows.

More and more, Aquarian values make themselves felt in the world. "Either-or" polarities are no longer clear. The middle, under attack or ignored for so long, is beginning to be respected. Gray areas are now seen as valid. A new subtlety enters the world. The hard line is no longer viable; the middle ground has become interesting.

The Tarot opens us to our inner worlds wherein dwell heaven and hell, the light and the shadow. There is no better tool for viewing the shadow than the Tarot. The unconscious speaks through dreams, and the Tarot is dreaming awake.

My own experience with the Tarot is that it will bring you into crisis. How can it not? As your views on life and others change, your relationships will change. Old views will be challenged, but you must persist. *There is no growth without crisis.* However, as understanding of self and others develops, the state of crisis becomes less devastating.

Through the Tarot we develop our ability to see "what is," which often includes both what we would like to be and what is actually happening in our relationships. With this information our lives begin to manifest the consciousness that enables us to make clear judgments untrammeled by dreamy self-interest. Our lives become harmonious. We begin to manifest tranquility and wisdom. We come into balance; and the world comes into balance.

Love and light,
Peter Balin
Author of *The Flight of
Feathered Serpent*
Hollywood, California

Part 1

Tarot—Your Living Canvas

Tarot Tutor 1

This short section appearing at the beginning of each of the six parts of the book briefly highlights the theme of that part.

In Part 1, Chapter 1, we introduce you to the Tarot and to the Celtic Cross spread on which the Tarot for Two is based. Chapter 2 clarifies what your Tarot for Two readings can do that traditional readings do not.

Nothing looks more benign than a Tarot deck that is facedown, neatly stacked. Some take the cards lightly, as a game. Others would— and probably have—gladly let the Tarot organize their entire life. Historically, bitter arguments have erupted over the meanings of the cards and their order of arrangement. Debates raged about whether or not the Tarot was the carrier of ancient mysteries and, if it was, then just exactly to whom these mysteries should be revealed.

The first deck we know of began as art, painted in Italy. Since that time hundreds of people have painted or created decks. There is no doubt that in a variety of ways Tarot stimulates creativity.

Now it is your turn. We view Tarot spreads as works of art depicting some aspect of your life relationships. We think that shuffling and shifting the cards, and the momentary reverie you slip into as you focus on your intent, reorder your mind as surely as they reorder the cards. Your inner canvas prepares for its unveiling.

Guided by your need for answers, your higher wisdom probes the dusky cubbyholes of your memory, unlatches the doors of your personal symbology, and ultimately delivers up to the daylight your heartfelt inner canvas, your Tarotscape.

Through the language of the cards, your Tarotscapes—as we call the completed spreads—give you a new perspective, new ideas to consider. A thoughtfully constructed Tarotscape acts not only as a reflection, but also as an inspiration. Its scene enables you to examine your relationships in a specific way and stimulates you to think about your situation in ways you might not have otherwise.

So, ready, everyone? Let's paint.

Chapter 1
The Inspiration

Although there are a number of lovely and intriguing stories about the origin of the Tarot, its actual beginnings are buried in obscurity. Whether, as some say, it is legendary (the secret wisdom of Atlantis) or merely ancient (descended from the Egyptians), its appearance in the form of cards can only be historically documented from the fifteenth-century Visconti deck, painted in Italy.

During the nineteenth century, esotericists and artists actively extended the Tarot tradition. Eliphas Levi connected the Tarot to the cabala of Jewish mysticism. A number of new decks were designed and painted, notably the Rider-Waite deck, designed by Arthur Edward Waite and painted by Pamela Colman Smith, and the Thoth deck, designed by Aleister Crowley and painted by Lady Frieda Harris.

Along the limbs of this ancestral tree, major differences budded concerning how Tarot cards should be used, who should use them, and what a Tarot reading was all about. Some regard readings as akin to Gypsy fortune-telling, with all the positive benefits that implies if you are a believer, or with all its silly or negative aspects if you are a cynic. Believers in the Gypsy theory often regard Gypsies as the inheritors and carriers of ancient Egyptian mysteries, although there is no real evidence of that.

More and more modern Tarot readers and authors are coming to regard a Tarot reading as not necessarily predictive, but, rather, as offering another viewpoint, a different message, which may aid in the decision-making process.

The more psychologically minded also consider that, in addition, the symbols on the cards may stimulate our conscious and unconscious motifs, helping us to clarify wisps of ideas still forming at the tips of our minds. Personal responses—stimulation—to a card's symbols are one of the reasons that one deck often speaks more clearly to us than another.

We like to think of Tarot spreads as the artful expression of your life, your living canvas. Keeping a record of your layouts is like an artist painting a series to show or express the transformation of an idea. Separately, each layout presents a unique perspective or issue, a translation into the visible of some aspect of your inner being. They express what Wassily Kandinsky, the father of abstract art, called "inner ripenings."[1]

Together, all our layouts—our Tarotscapes—say more than each can express separately. They depict our personal search for harmony and balance. With the Tarot we are all artists, living our relationships and painting the canvases of our lives. We bring our cosmic essence into awareness and express the artistic creation that is our unique life.

Getting to Know Your New Deck

If you do not already own a Tarot deck, you can purchase decks at most metaphysical or occult bookstores. Some large or national bookstore chains now carry Tarot cards, reflecting their increasing popularity.

Tarot decks also can be ordered from U.S. Games Systems, Inc., 170 Ludlow Street, Stamford, CT 06902. Their "Best of Cards Catalog" lists hundreds of decks and related books.

Most Tarot decks provide a booklet of instructions which includes meanings or symbols for each card and one or more examples of a layout, usually accompanied by tips for reading or understanding the layout.

Books for the beginner which delve into the meanings of the Rider-Waite cards—the deck we use for relationship issues—include those by Sidney Bennett,[2] Eileen Connolly,[3] Eden Gray,[4] David LeMieux,[5] Rachel Pollack,[6] and, of course, Arthur Waite himself.[7] Many of the books in our bibliography include interpretations for other decks.

Most decks are divided traditionally into a Major Arcana and a Minor Arcana. The 22 Major Arcana cards represent the higher energies of focused attention, sometimes referred to as archetypal or spiritual energies, which each of us possesses in our psychological makeup.

Reflecting inner strengths, these energies symbolize steppingstones on the pathway toward awakening higher consciousness.[8] When we con-

---

[1] *Kandinsky: Complete Writings on Art*, 1982.
[2] *Tarot for the Millions*, 1967.
[3] *Tarot. A New Handbook for the Journeyman*, 1979.
[4] *The Tarot Revealed*, 1960, and *Mastering the Tarot*, 1971.
[5] *Forbidden Images*, 1985.
[6] *Seventy-Eight Degrees of Wisdom, Parts I and 2*, 1980 and 1983.
[7] *The Pictorial Key to the Tarot*, 1971 and 1986.
[8] Rachel Pollack, *Seventy-Eight Degrees of Wisdom. Part I: The Major Arcana*, 1980.

sciously work with the cards, especially in meditation, we expand our focus and therefore our choices and our personal power for dealing with life situations. In this sense the Tarot acts as a gateway for widening our vision. It allows us to paint pictures with more depth.

The 56 Minor Arcana cards reflect our outer experiences, daily situations and struggles, or activities that we are exposed to frequently. They represent our personal beliefs and attitudes, our sense of security and self-esteem. For Jungian scholar Stephan Hoeller, the Minor Arcana cards symbolically stand for the lower self, or personality of man.[9] Reflecting our public and private selves, they show the everyday stuff of everyday life.

At times Major Arcana cards also can represent mundane (everyday) situations involving people, aspects, or qualities of our question, or of ourselves. Often these are circumstances we have not recognized, or side issues toward which we have directed little attention.

Determining whether the message of any individual card of the Major Arcana is mundane or spiritual depends on:

- the card's position in the layout
- the other cards in the layout
- the nature of the question
- your skill and experience in working with the cards.

Taken together, the Tarot deck comprises a "universal language formed in the collective unconscious of the human race."[10] Understanding this language helps you explore the dimensions of your own Tarotscapes as well as those of others.

We suggest you use the Rider-Waite deck to begin learning the Tarot and exploring your relationships because:

1. The complete deck of 78 cards is available in three sizes and the Tarot for Two layout uses decks of two different sizes or shapes.
2. There is more general commentary and interpretive material available for this deck than for any other single deck.
3. The descriptive scenes on each of the 56 Minor Arcana cards offer additional opportunity for you to learn and practice symbolic interpretation.

Once you have acquired your decks, use the four exercises that follow to get acquainted with your cards. For future reference, you may

---

[9]*The Royal Road,* 1975.
[10]Craig Junjulas, *Psychic Tarot,* 1985, p. 6.

wish to record your responses to these and additional exercises in a notebook or three-ring binder.

Using a notebook allows you to log your progress, recording and tracking:

- growth in your personal skills in Tarot reading
- the developmental sequence of your relationships
- supplemental information gleaned from accessory spreads (Chapters 17 and 18).

Later you may want to label separate sections of your binder for each kind of relationship you explore: family, romance, love, children, work, religious or spiritual, self (inner growth).

Exercise 1—Getting to Know Your New Deck: Before you read any interpretations of card meanings, write down a description of each card as you see it—what the card says to you.

Comparing your descriptions to standard descriptions helps you become aware of your own personal symbolic ideas.

Exercise 2—Learning Your Emotional Reactions to a New Deck: Set aside an uninterrupted time to look at each card one at a time, paying attention to any feelings, memories, or even physical sensations it evokes.

Jot down your reactions in your notebook. Often they change as you continue working with the cards. A record of these changes may reflect personal changes or developing insight.

Exercise 3—Creating Stories for the Cards in a New Deck: Before you read any interpretation of the cards, go through them one at a time, making up a story about what's happening in each scene and writing it in your notebook.

Exercise 4—Combining Standard Meanings with Your Reactions: To learn and combine the standard meanings of the cards with your own insights, read through the meanings for all the cards in the booklet that comes with your deck.

Put it aside. Look at the cards one at a time, then write what you remember about the meaning of the card, adding your own reactions from previous exercises or new meanings that occur during this exercise.

Meditating on a card is another way to become acquainted with its symbology and energy. Connolly,[11] Hoeller,[12] Pollack,[13] and Edwin Steinbrecher[14] all suggest ways this can be done.

The more you work with any one card, the more intimate you become with it. Its images may stir up memories of actual or imagined situations from your past.

Although most of us have only read or seen movies about some of the actions pictured—knights brandishing swords, fair maidens taming lions, queens reigning from thrones—they may, nevertheless, seem as real to us as if we were in them now. Paying attention to our feelings and reactions about card actions can spur us to recall how we dealt with analogous situations in our own lives and can promote insight into our next steps for personal growth.

Our reactions to cards sometimes reflect aspects of ourselves we may or may not have dealt with.[15] If a card depicts a situation that makes you feel uncomfortable, it may be showing you something about yourself that you do not understand, have not explored, or are rejecting.

For instance, the Rider-Waite Five of Swords shows a young man in the foreground, smiling and holding swords. Another person in the distance has his head down; a third person walks away.

If you identify yourself as the foreground youth, perhaps picking up what others have lost or left behind, become aware of the feelings this evokes. Is it victory? Is it guilt? Or perhaps it's greed ("I've got more swords than you have"). How do you deal with those feelings in comparable daily life situations?

If you identify with the person in apparent despair or with the person walking away, how does that apply to your relationship situations?

If we let them, Tarot cards will provoke into awareness some aspect of our inner psychological development[16] or our personal mythology. They have the potential to "unlock all the mysteries of life."[17]

---

[11] *Tarot. A New Handbook for the Journeyman,* 1979.

[12] *The Royal Road,* 1975.

[13] *The Open Labyrinth,* 1986.

[14] *The Inner Guide Meditation,* 1970.

[15] Rachel Pollack, *Salvador Dali's Tarot,* 1985.

[16] Craig Junjulas, *Psychic Tarot,* 1985.

[17] Sidney Bennett, *Tarot for the Millions,* 1967, p. 11.

Basic Celtic Cross Spread

The Celtic Cross spread (see Figure 1), if not one of the oldest, is certainly the best-known layout used in reading Tarot cards. Many Tarot experts believe it dates from the Middle Ages, while others say only from the nineteenth century.

The spread has two parts:

1. The cross, which consists of two center cards—one vertical and one horizontal—and one card on each of the four sides, forming the arms of the cross.

2. The staff. Laid out to the right of the cross, it is created by placing four cards in a vertical row, one above the other, proceeding from bottom to top.

A total of 10 cards is used. Authors differ as to the various names of the positions and the sequences given to arrive at the Celtic Cross layout. The instruction booklet accompanying the Rider-Waite deck suggests selecting a significator card (a card that represents the person) before shuffling the deck. This selection influences the shuffling, the cards drawn, and, ultimately, the entire reading. The first card drawn for the actual reading is then designated as covering the significator and is laid down over it.[18]

The second card drawn is laid across the first, creating a miniature cross at the center of the larger cross. Pollack, among others, believes the "micro-cross" tells the whole story, while the other cards in the spread fill in the details.

The Celtic Cross spread seeks to answer a question by examining the attitudes, beliefs, and motivations of the person with the question—commonly called the querent by Tarot readers. Cards in the cross explore elements of the question and its dynamics. Staff cards reflect energies and resources available for support.

The Tarot for Two uses the framework of the Celtic Cross but modifies the meanings of the positions, which we call heartprints, so they more accurately reflect personality and relationship issues. Table 1 shows how the more commonly used names and meanings of the Celtic Cross positions have been changed to deal with relationship issues in the new Tarot for Two heartprints.

---

[18]In the Tarot for Two spread we combine those first two cards into the Where am I? position.

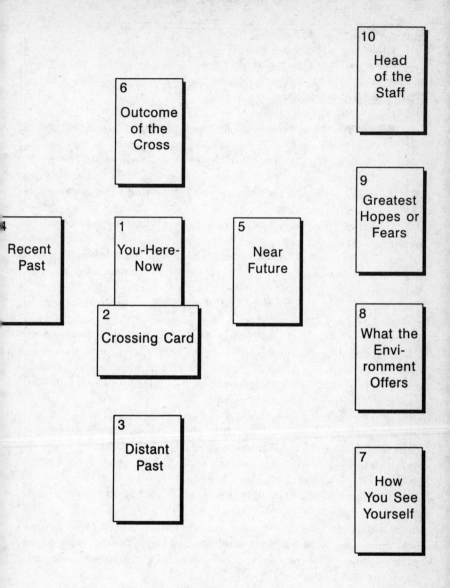

Figure 1
Basic Celtic Cross Spread

Table 1
Tarot for Two Heartprint Changes
in
Celtic Cross Positions

Position Number	Celtic Cross Positions	Tarot for Two Heartprints
1	You-Here-Now	Where am I?
2	Crossing	What's in my way?
3	Distant Past	Where have I been?
4	Recent Past	What's been happening?
5	Near Future	What's in store for me?
6	Outcome of the Cross	What are my options?
7	How You See Yourself	Who do I think I am?
8	What the Environment Offers	What's out there for me?
9	Greatest Hopes or Fears	What do I expect?
10	Head of the Staff	Where does all this lead?
11		What else is new?[19]

---

[19]Optional Tarot for Two heartprint. No comparable Celtic Cross position.

Chapter 2
The Picture Does Its Work

The history of peoples past and present—our history—is the story of relationships. From our beginning days, both as a species and as individuals, we have striven to find and take our place within our world, our tribes or ethnic groups, as well as within our families, communities, and professions.

For those of us living today, that is no less true than for our ancestors, even though the society in which we live is far more complex. All the more reason for developing a means to understand, and work successfully within, our relationships.

While many people—especially those who do not draw upon Tarot wisdom—think that Tarot cards are only used for divination, we believe that is not necessarily the best way to use them.

Whether done for one or more persons, all Tarot readings really concern our relationships. Even when we use the cards to seek information solely about ourselves, we are asking questions about what psychologists call our "self-relationship," our relationship with various aspects of ourself.

So why, you may ask, do we need a new spread for relationships? Why can't we just get information about our relationships from a regular Tarot reading?

Tarot for Two establishes different boundaries—a new canvas—from which to view your relationship issues. Psychologists call this "reframing," a shift in perspective that frees you to make new choices and decisions.

Specific cards in specific positions—we call them heartprints in the Tarot for Two layout—act as pathways through which you can examine your various partnerings. Not only do you create your Tarotscapes, but you can also explore their depths.

Although Tarot for Two is more complex than single readings, we created specific questions to guide you through each heartprint of your Tarotscape. They help you, working alone or with your partner, to see both sides of a situation and to combine that into an explanation of interaction.

Part of the Tarot for Two's effectiveness lies in suggesting new directions and options for your consideration and in helping you create ideas for resolving your relationship issues. It offers you information in a provocative form and, when you are working with another, stimulates planning for a mutually agreed-on way of combining your differences.

Paraphrasing television's homicide detective Sgt. Rick Hunter, "It worked for us" as we planned and wrote this book. From time to time we needed insight into our working relationship. During one reading, one of us drew the Eight of Swords and the other drew The Devil, Major Arcana XV, for the heartprint that raises the question What's out there for me?

We identified the Eight of Sword's person as not seeing available choices, having a limited view. The other, represented by The Devil card, had an illusory perception about our working relationship, was not seeing it realistically.

The two cards showed we weren't talking about the same project. We redefined it so we were in agreement and were working toward the same goals.

A Tarot for Two reading provides new ground for candid communication and offers a win/win situation for examining various facets of your relationship. According to your own comfort, you can use information from the cards to examine conditioning and opinions or prejudices affecting the issue. Quite often a Tarotscape highlights what each partner has been ignoring or neglecting, including possible sexual needs if appropriate.

Doing a Tarot for Two without your partner enables you to take a different, more objective viewpoint about the other's position. Certainly if your partner is a person, rather than a project or an idea, your expanded perspective may offer the perfect opportunity to open a new dialogue or to interact in a different way.

If your Tarotscape evokes ideas and emotions and awakens your imagination, then, like an inspiring painting, it has done its work. It has sparked your "in-sight."

The Book Does Its Work

Special features that make *The Lovers' Tarot* easy to use and the creation of Tarotscapes easy to learn include:

- Exercises to help you learn about your Tarot cards and the Tarot for Two.
- A blank Tarot for Two Tarotscape form (Appendix 1), which can be duplicated, enabling you to see your Tarotscapes at a glance and to keep sequential records for review.
- A set of three worksheets (Chapter 13 and Appendix 1) and a series of questions (Chapter 11 and Appendix 2) to photocopy and use to get the most out of your Tarot for Two readings.
- Instructions for four new spreads and a ritual mandala—with blank forms in Appendix 1—to help you monitor the progress of your relationships.

Part 2

Priming the Canvas

Tarot Tutor 2

Engaging in Tarot for Two readings and creating Tarotscapes offer you a framework for delving into the basic, too often hidden question at the core of every Tarot reading: "What is really going on in my relationship with . . . (fill in the blank)?" Filling in that blank with exquisite detail is what a Tarotscape is all about.

The nucleus of any Tarotscape is the Tarot cards—the tools you use to liberate your inner pictures and transform them into your outer canvas. Understanding their revelations is a major step in creating and exploring your Tarotscapes.

Card meanings as they apply to relationships are recounted in Chapters 3 (Major Arcana) and 4 (Minor Arcana). Chapter 5 guides you in refining and expanding card concepts.

This section might be likened to an art course on meeting the masters. After understanding the spirit they infused into their paintings and the techniques they used to express subtle concepts, never again can you cast a virgin view at a Rembrandt, a Monet—or a Queen of Swords.

Eager for finesse? Have your cards handy as we peruse the gallery of images that will soon permeate your own Tarotscapes.

Chapter 3

Transformative Images

It's in the Cards

Using the Tarot to explore relationships is really not new. In fact, relationships are an integral quality of the cards themselves.

Several authors have explored relationships within the Major Arcana cards and created stories or concepts about what certain sequences reveal.

Rachel Pollack suggests that by arranging the Major Arcana, minus The Fool, in three rows of seven each (seven represents victory), they symbolically express the three levels of challenges we all face in our personal development:

1. the ordinary problems of our daily relationships
2. the inward work of spiritual development, which can culminate in
3. our joining with archetypal forces.

The Fool, "who cannot be pinned down,"[20] provides us with courage to continue.

P. D. Ouspensky combined the cards in a specific triangular and rectangular pattern to depict the relationship between God (the world of ideas), the universe or physical world, and man, the realm of the soul. Peter Balin, creator of the Xultun deck, translates this into the relationship between the nagual (the world of the mysterious unknown), the tonal (the world of form), and our individual consciousness.

Stuart Kaplan[21] says each *suit* sequence of the Rider-Waite deck presents a different but continuous story about family life and values, although we have yet to find any reference in Waite's own writings. Our work in delving into the meaning of the suit of Swords (see Chapter 4) suggests each suit carries its own sequence of ideas. Rather than having to memorize separate card meanings, if you create such a sequence for yourself, it will serve as your own mnemonic device.

---

[20]Rachel Pollack, *Salvador Dali's Tarot,* 1985, p. 9.

[21]*The Encyclopedia of Tarot,* Vol. I, 1978.

Finally, we want to remind you that although cards are first read and interpreted individually, in an actual Tarot for Two reading they are never considered in isolation, but rather—you knew we were going to say this—in relationship to one another. Each card's message is modified by its heartprint position and its relation to the other cards in the layout, as you will see when you create your own Tarotscapes.

Archetypal Mysteries: Major Arcana

The word "arcana" means secrets or mysteries. There are 22 cards in the Major Arcana, but "Major" doesn't refer to the secrets we all have locked away or the mysteries young Nancy Drew can't avoid. Rather, it refers to the kinds of secrets or mysteries that are so potent they act as major keys or steppingstones in our journey toward inner growth and spiritual development. In earlier times they were passed along only to initiates by tribal or temple priests.

These secrets have also been called archetypal patterns of behavior, states of consciousness inherent in us all, and "higher" potentials for self-perfection. While none of the cards in a Tarotscape can be disregarded, when Major Arcana cards appear, they are like the light of a brilliant beacon which should not be ignored.

Because of the endless variety of questions we humans can contrive, the relationship meaning for each Major Arcana card may not always seem to fit your question exactly. So, following the narrative meanings for each card, we provide a list of key words and phrases. They offer you additional concepts and facilitate quick interpretation.

We also have added blank lines after the meanings of each card so you can insert your own understandings, gleaned, perhaps, from the exercises in other chapters in this book.

THE FOOL .

THE FOOL
0 OR XXII (22)

That facet of yourself which is The Fool appears as a traveler, always on the go, full of the adventure of life. A child of the universe, The Fool is optimistic, open to new ideas, and makes choices without fear or reservation, although sometimes these decisions are regarded as foolhardy by others.

When we are on a seeking quest, whether for personal or universal truths, for quick answers, or for just plain fun, we are acting from our inner Fool. We do not always need to reach a goal. The search itself may be satisfying, nurturing, or healing.

Even though we may have been battered by life, The Fool card represents our innocent and childlike attitudes, remnants of which still remain within us to be awakened, or drawn upon, when appropriate.

Unafraid of the unknown, The Fool may stumble rather innocently into a relationship without too much forethought, bringing spontaneity and a kind of erotic vitality, but also a reluctance to commit and a carefreeness that will be seen by some as irresponsible. Unfortunately, our fearless Fool has a capacity to be oblivious and unaware of the deepening of the relationship, as well as of developing problems.

In relationship issues The Fool may signify that you are at a place where you know nothing (a kind of innocence) and need help. Since that recognition is often the first step in accepting guidance, in whatever form it arrives, this card may also signify that help is on the way—possibly through the Tarot for Two reading itself. Therefore, be especially alert to the heartprint in which The Fool appears and to the cards which follow it.

KEY WORDS AND PHRASES: traveler; adventure of life; reluctance to commit; optimism; open to new ideas; erotic vitality; child of the universe; choice without fear; innocence; purity; unknown; not responsible; unaware.

_____

_____

_____

_____

_____

THE MAGICIAN.

I—THE MAGICIAN

How could we accomplish anything without The Magician, who represents our ability to make choices, to be creative, and to use our initiative? It is from our Magician within that we derive confidence in our skills and abilities and the tenacity or focus to practice and develop new skills.

The Magician is a unifier. Naturally intuitive or sensitive to possibilities, he thrives on bringing people and their ideas together for creative purposes.

If The Magician has a like-minded partner, together they will dedicate themselves to transforming their relationship into something more meaningful than either of them would have alone. They learn the "laws" of creating a relationship and practice applying them.

Although our inner Magician represents masculine sexual vitality, when this archetypal energy is active for men or women, we are also quite capable of sublimating sexual energy to focus on business or other projects.

When we are concerned with understanding or exploring the link between something apparent and something obscure—say between the spiritual world and the material world, or between the inner and outer person—that is The Magician acting within us.

This card gives the go-ahead for accomplishment on all levels.

KEY WORDS AND PHRASES: unity; masculine sexual vitality; ability to sublimate sexual energy; ability to choose; creative; focused will; initiative; ability to manifest; confidence; linking of the spiritual and the material, of inner and outer; abilities; skill through practice.

_____
_____
_____
_____
_____

THE HIGH PRIESTESS

II—THE HIGH PRIESTESS

Composed on her throne, The High Priestess unveils feminine wisdom and mature feminine sexuality. A lover of mystery and the hidden, The High Priestess within us traditionally represents the unconscious and inner knowledge. When our archetypal High Priestess energy is activated, we often have the sense of being directed by an inner guide. At those times we may be more intuitive than usual.

Drawing this card can serve as a signal that you may soon become more aware of earlier memories or conflicts.

Our inner High Priestess often influences our actions in ways we may not be aware of. In that sense she can also represent the veiled law: the conditioning (automatic responses) of early years or training and the influence of repressed or forgotten incidents.

While we are all unaware of many of our motivations, we may deliberately hide those of which we *are* aware from certain others when our High Priestess is active.

KEY WORDS AND PHRASES: duality; hidden motivations; well-developed feminine sexuality; the unconscious; feminine wisdom; intuition; silence; mystery (hidden influences); conditioning.

_____

_____

_____

_____

_____

THE EMPRESS.

III—THE EMPRESS

The Empress archetype is one of personal synthesis, creativity, and abundance. When inner Empress energy is activated, we are able to trust the wisdom of our hearts and, if we are in an authority position, to be nurturing and compassionate.

The Empress represents feminine sexual vitality, motherhood, and fertility, not only of body, but of ideas as well. She is the quintessential creator of peace and harmony, even though she will encourage and sometimes lovingly nudge her mate and her offspring—whether they be children or ideas—toward growth and fruition.

When The Empress occurs in a layout, welcome the opportunity for productive action. You are—or soon will be, depending on the position—in harmony instinctually, mentally, and spiritually.

KEY WORDS AND PHRASES: creativity; nurturing authority;

feminine sexual vitality and fertility; synthesis; abundance; motherhood; fruitfulness; wisdom of the heart.

_____
_____
_____
_____
_____

THE EMPEROR.

IV—THE EMPEROR

The archetype of masculine authority, leadership, and fatherhood, The Emperor is ambitious and a good manager of his affairs. He has mature sexual values and mastery and is well able to assume responsibility in business and in the family. He is considered a stable and contributing member of his community and of civic or professional organizations.

Whether we are male or female, when our Emperor energy is active, we rely more on reason than on emotion for guidance in decision making. We can be very aggressive and forceful, even stubborn ("Do it my way"), in trying to make our points.

Our inner Emperor allows us to be disciplined enough to carry through projects or reach our goals. On the other hand, our Emperor energy can be very rigid in defining or applying rules and unhesitant in chastising ourselves or others for failure to abide by those rules.

The Emperor shows who is providing the structure for interaction in the relationship and/or protecting the relationship from outside disruption.

KEY WORDS AND PHRASES: foundation; assumption of authority; sexual mastery; father; lawmaker; reason; sight; strength; responsibility; discipline; mental activity; aggression; "Do it my way."

_____

_____

_____

_____

_____

V—THE HIEROPHANT

The quintessential teacher, at his best The Hierophant represents selflessness guided by higher values. Spiritual initiative, sometimes expressed or recognized by us as the voice of our inner teacher, is active Hierophant energy. At this time we may be directed toward spiritual study and initiation or personal growth. When our inner Hierophant is active, we are also concerned with attending to traditional values and honoring our heritage.

In its negative sense The Hierophant archetype can be severe and demanding, urging us to conform to peer pressure. When we unquestioningly accept the precepts of any social institution without being clear that we are *choosing* them, that is Hierophant activity in its most rigid form.

The Hierophant card shows which person in the relationship is operating under conventional patterns. It can also identify a partner who has learned important interpersonal lessons that can be infused into the present relationship.

KEY WORDS AND PHRASES: teacher; spiritual initiative; selfless; higher values; inner hearing; mercy; inner teacher; education; organized religion; conformity; peer pressure; severity.

_____

_____

_____

_____

_____

VI—THE LOVERS

The Lovers card expresses a time of openness, communication, and sexual freedom as a couple. When The Lovers archetype is active within us, we have a sense of integration of the spiritual, mental, and physical. We feel whole as all aspects of ourselves actively interact and balance one another. Naturally, a sense of harmony and completion results from this coordination.

Our inner Lovers are functioning when we have a sense of doing and caring for others, offering them support. The Lovers archetype derives in part from the internalization of both benevolent maternal and paternal attitudes.

Operating from our Lovers archetype allows us to face adventures or attend to business knowing we possess a haven and will not be overwhelmed. Our wounds will be cared for and we will be nurtured. This does not necessarily refer to a mate or a particular home. It can also refer to the sense of security, the safe harbor, which we derive from our inner self or our unconscious.

Appearing in a couple's Tarotscape, this card can signify a union that is "made in heaven." It also suggests joint aspirations and the desire to unite minds and actions to meet these goals. Both the working toward unity and its successful completion—which is indicated by this card—will create a sense of harmony.

KEY WORDS AND PHRASES: love; openness; communication; sexual freedom together; spiritual trinity (conscious, unconscious, and higher self); integration of spiritual and physical; wholeness; harmony; completion; union; joint aspirations.

THE CHARIOT.

VII—THE CHARIOT

The Chariot shows strong motivation toward resolution of the question. For couples, this card indicates they are pulling together toward their goals and success is in the picture.

The Chariot archetype conveys high adventure as well as important mental journeys. It is a time when we can let our higher self be "in the driver's seat," and a time when there is a good balance between our conscious and unconscious forces.

Behaving from our Chariot archetype, we have a sense of progress, feel good about ourselves, and may take more risks than usual. The Chariot also indicates sexual prowess and victories.

KEY WORDS AND PHRASES: success; pulling together; sexual prowess; sexual victories; high adventure; balance of conscious and unconscious forces; awareness of human nature; spiritual movement;

letting the higher self be in the driver's seat; mental journeys; progress; self-esteem; risk-taking.

_____

_____

_____

_____

VIII—STRENGTH

The Strength card announces the availability of courage and perseverance for help in overcoming our problems.

The Strength archetype allows us to gather our energies for the next stage in our development as a person or as a couple, and gives us the courage to take that step. Sexually it can indicate the "taming" of the physical and sexual nature, or transmuting physical energy into spiritual.

When we are able to blend, or are working to come to some stability between active and passive aspects of ourselves or our coupling, our Strength archetype is active.

Drawing this card signals a sense of confidence in, and consideration for, the ideas or activities of another.

KEY WORDS AND PHRASES: courage; taming of physical and sexual nature; considering the other; transmuting physical to spiritual; sense of the eternal; confidence; conscious blending of passive and active forces; gathering energies for perfection.

_____

_____

_____

THE HERMIT.

IX—THE HERMIT

The Hermit archetype highlights the wisdom and compassion we gain from our life experiences. Depending on your philosophical or spiritual bent, when The Hermit within is active, you may have a sense of attending to your conscience, your guardian angel, your deity, or your higher wisdom.

Sometimes we have withdrawn from relationships for a period of time in order to heal, to attain some wisdom or perspective about our experiences, or to develop the next chapter in our philosophy of being. Ultimately, however, we are called back to the real world, the world of relationships, to put what we have learned or resolved into practice.

So, depending on where you are in your growth, personally or within a relationship, The Hermit can represent a sense of detachment or isolation, a temporary need for healing retreat, or the time to return and share your new wisdom with others.

KEYWORDS AND PHRASES: inner light; wisdom of experience; attainment; philosopher; healer; compassion; sexual mastery; sharing experiences; maturity; role model; temporary withdrawal from relationship; detachment; isolation.

X—WHEEL OF FORTUNE

Is your relationship in an "up" or "down" phase? Are you reaping the rewards or the damage from previous behaviors or attitudes, cause and effect in action? The Wheel of Fortune archetype reminds us that life and relationships are cyclic.

In its positive sense this card reminds us it is time to take stock of our resources and use some which we may have been overlooking. Or it may be time to learn something new which will give you or your relationship fresh vitality.

The card can signify that one phase of a relationship is ending—has ended or will soon end, depending on the heartprint in which it falls—and a new one is beginning. It can also suggest a loss of purpose in the relationship.

When our inner Wheel of Fortune is active, we may be acutely sensitive to our own or another's inner timing and can plan our communications and interactions accordingly. Awareness of cycles—our own or another's—lets us have a sense of hope and the willingness to trust and wait for the next phase of the cycle.

KEY WORDS AND PHRASES: cycles; change; need for movement; timing; destiny; luck; hope; cause and effect; recognition and use of resources; ups and downs of life; seeking new purpose in the relationship; learning something new.

_____

_____

_____

_____

_____

XI—JUSTICE

When the archetype of Justice operates within an individual or a relationship, stability and equity reign. If the relationship is not already one of fairness and equality, then the card signifies that we as individuals will expect these qualities and will work within our relationships to develop them, or will need to work toward these ideals. Justice can also signify sexual equality in the relationship.

Social manners, consideration, ethical values, and legal matters are important for the Justice person or relationship. When you draw Justice, it may be a signal that your issue or project is—or needs to be—concerned with the rights of others.

When our inner Justice is active, we are ready to take responsibility based on our ethical beliefs and to seek balance within ourselves or the relationship.

KEYWORDS AND PHRASES: balance; equity; administration of law; value; ideal; legal matters; education; ethical values; stability in relationships; action/reaction; taking responsibility; seeking balance, fairness, or equality in the relationship; sexual equality.

_____
_____
_____
_____
_____

XII—THE HANGED MAN

The Hanged Man calls for a change in outlook and approach to the issue or problem. We are able to see others' viewpoints when our inner Hanged Man is active. In this sense The Hanged Man represents the kind of insight or clear sight which allows us to change our position toward the relationship or issue with confidence that we will attain something better. For those who are religious or spiritually inclined, it may signify a time of spiritual surrender and acceptance.

The Hanged Man raises the question of whether we have our values reversed. We may need to consider our priorities and perhaps reorder them for the sake of our personal integrity or for the success of the relationship.

When you draw this card, it's time to get out of your rut. Step back from your preconceived notions and take another viewpoint—even if only temporarily—to consider the issue and obtain new information.

The card can also denote idealized sexuality, an alternative sexual lifestyle, or a sexual transition.

KEY WORDS AND PHRASES: reversal; change in outlook and approach; clear sight; seeing the other's viewpoint; reversed values; spiritual surrender; prophetic vision; open to change; idealized sexuality; alternative sexual lifestyle.

_____

_____

_____

_____

_____

XIII—DEATH

The archetypal meaning of this card is CHANGE: time for a change, time to reconsider. Change is imminent. Now is not the time to dig in your heels and stick to what you believe.

We are willing to consider letting go of the old and facing a new beginning when our Death archetype is active. This card does not necessarily signify the end of the relationship, although it can, but rather the end of a particular way of being within that relationship—the transforming of ourselves or the relationship into something different. It can also indicate new sexual expression or the end of sexual naïveté.

Changes, even those we consider positive and willingly embrace, often feel like a loss. We leave behind a part of ourselves. The Death card reminds us to take sufficient time to mourn or to acknowledge the ending of the old ways so we can face the new with fresh attitudes and energy, as if reborn.

KEY WORDS AND PHRASES: change; transformation; release; rebirth; accepting changes; regeneration; letting go of things; new beginnings; new sexual expression; end of sexual naïveté.

_____
_____
_____
_____
_____

XIV—TEMPERANCE

Balance and harmony prevail when the archetype of Temperance operates within you or your relationship. You have a sense of inner peace and understanding. Temperance may also signify that you have successfully balanced the spiritual and the material within your ideals or within the relationship. It can indicate that your sexual needs and behaviors are balanced.

During Temperance times you interact without strain and are able to blend your separate individualities to strengthen the relationship. You may arrive at a new understanding of your own inner workings or those of your relationship. You, as a couple or as individuals, carefully consider and choose with care.

When your inner Temperance is active, it is easy for you to consider both sides of an issue or to compromise without losing your integrity.

KEY WORDS AND PHRASES: harmony; balance of spiritual and material; inner peace; modification; understanding; blending; higher learning; choosing with care; interaction; considering both sides; compromise; balance of sexual desires and behaviors.

_____

_____

_____

_____

_____

XV—THE DEVIL

The Devil archetype underscores our battles with illusion. The word "devil" derives from the Greek *diabolos*, which merely means adversary.

In its most positive sense it is our inner Devil which calls for us to recognize our limitations, and to laugh at them if need be. It allows us to see another's real value, no matter the facade or mask that the person presents.

In another sense The Devil card can signal compulsive clinging to a particular value or position—self-imposed bondage, so to speak. It suggests that we are blocked and fearful, unable to accept or acknowledge available ideas, resources, or inner knowledge.

When our inner Devil is operating in this fashion, we are likely to mix up our mate's behavior with that of a parent or someone from a previous relationship. We ignore his or her individuality and specialness and compress our perspective: "You're just like all men." . . . "Women, that's the way they are." . . . "You sound just like my father [or mother, or ex-mate]."

Locking into our bedeviled behaviors or viewpoints often creates confusion and misunderstanding for everyone. Zealously clinging to singular attitudes or beliefs can ultimately destroy a relationship. The Devil card calls upon you to come out from behind your bleak clouds and adopt a different approach.

As couples, we must develop what works for us, rather than clinging to the sometimes illusory "security" learned from dysfunctional parents, or to values resulting from, say, abusive situations. It may be time to ask, "Whose idea is this, anyway? Where, or how, did I get it? Do I really believe this or want to keep operating from this perspective?"

KEY WORDS AND PHRASES: illusion; seeing through limitations; laughing at illusion; seeing one another's real value; misunderstanding; compulsion; ignorance; self-imposed bondage; blockage; fear; "Whose idea is this?"; something sexually kinky.

_____

_____

_____

_____

_____

THE TOWER.

XVI—THE TOWER

Translate The Tower as unexpected circumstances, or abrupt changes of opinions or attitudes, that call for us to adapt or adjust. It is a time when we need support from our mate or others.

When The Tower archetype is active in our relationship, we can expect the appearance of a catalyst to stir things up. Is an outside challenge shaking or threatening your relationship, or is it internal? Will we receive that impetus as one promoting conflict and destruction, or as a liberating factor which frees us from restriction and opens us to fresh viewpoints?

The relationship Tower is the structure we have built, especially the way we have boxed ourselves in. Hidden within its walls are decisions which didn't work, perhaps even a complete or well-ordered philosophy of how our relationship should work and doesn't. Let yourselves be catapulted into awareness as if suddenly struck by lightning.

This card can signal a need to pull together to redefine or rebuild the structure of your relationship. Release what no longer works. Fortify your direction; add or create new purpose; rebuild from strength.

KEY WORDS AND PHRASES: disruption; catalyst; unexpected challenges; abrupt changes of opinions and attitudes; necessary adaptation; need for support from mate or others; reversal; change in status quo; humbling of pride; conflict; destruction; "That didn't work."

_____
_____
_____
_____
_____

THE STAR.

XVII—THE STAR

The Star emits the glimmer of new trust in our relationships, possibly due to insights gained—truths revealed—after a time of meditation, thoughtfulness, or personal-growth work. Its appearance counsels taking a direct approach without manipulation.

When The Star is active within, we trust our inner direction, our guiding light. We freely give of ourselves with abundance, knowing that such giving will not deplete us. Our powers of expression are at their fullest potential. Sometimes this takes the form of activity. Sometimes we share new ideas; sometimes we simply serve as "a shining example."

Drawing this card can also indicate that help or insight is forthcoming.

KEY WORDS AND PHRASES: guide; meditation; truth revealed; inspiration; direction; abundance; hope; giving of yourself; endless supply; bright ideas; loss of false modesty; new trust in the relationship; a shining example.

_____

_____

_____

_____

_____

THE MOON.

XVIII—THE MOON

Instinct is a stronger or more active motivation than usual when you draw The Moon card. Although it is the archetype of feminine energy, The Moon also embodies cyclic changes in sexual energy for both men and women.

Because in many cultures the moon is a symbol of that which is hidden or dark, drawing this card identifies a time to tap into our unconscious, our intuition, and to use this information to make change.

Emerging feelings which occur when our inner Moon is active may take several forms: increased energy, painful memories surfacing, identifying fears that carry over from past relationships. Look to your dreams and slips of the tongue for clues.

In its best light The Moon suggests success in recognizing and accepting your animal nature or your personal demons. Seen from the dark side, The Moon indicates that if you do not integrate its insights, you will still be a person divided, unable to acknowledge your wholeness.

KEY WORDS AND PHRASES: reflection; magnetic feminine energy; cyclic; rhythmic; untapped power; change; unconscious intuition; influence on animal nature and emotion; feminine mystique; movement from the instinctual toward higher consciousness; change in sexual energy; time to reflect on each other's cycles—"Do our cycles match?"

_____

_____

_____

_____

XIX—THE SUN

The dynamic masculine energy of The Sun archetype encourages us to go forward, leaving the shadows behind.

When The Sun is active in our lives or our relationships, it is a time of new growth with shared happiness and renewed sexual energy or interest. We may need to play more to bring this about, or it may naturally follow, or be a part of, a period of regeneration in the relationship.

We often take leadership roles when our inner Sun is active, so The Sun also indicates a time of birthing and implementing new ideas or actions, a creative time. If we play the part of The Sun, we shine light on the situation. We can see in the light of day what may have been hidden by The Moon.

Where The Star gave us direction, The Sun gives us the illumination to accomplish what we want to do. It calls for us to listen to another person, or to reveal our own "in-lightened" knowledge about the project or relationship issue.

KEY WORDS AND PHRASES: consciousness; dynamic masculine energy; birth; regeneration; growth; light; creativity; magic; leadership; shared happiness; time for play; renewed sexual energy or interest.

_____

_____

_____

_____

_____

JUDGEMENT.

XX—JUDGEMENT

This card trumpets forth its archetypal meaning of liberation and transformation. It heralds a rise in consciousness, an access to wisdom that permits evaluation and frees us from previous illusion. We may have new insight into ourselves or our relationship, a sense of a new lease on life.

Inner Judgement directs us to heed our personal or sexual conscience. It can also indicate we may need to examine and acknowledge our values, discarding those that unduly prohibit us or cripple our effectiveness in relationships.

It calls for serious reevaluation according to higher values, dedicating ourselves to the awakening and acceptance of new possibilities. We are open to hearing the deep resonances from where we truly live.

KEY WORDS AND PHRASES: awakening; liberation; release from illusion; evaluation; heeding your sexual conscience; rise in consciousness; transformation; renewal; acceptance; karma; time to give up old attitudes; new insight into a relationship.

_____

_____

_____

THE WORLD.

XXI—THE WORLD

Synthesis, unification: we are The World, The World is us. When our inner World is active, we feel complete and whole, not bound or influenced by past experiences and conditioning. We often have the sense—and rightly so—that nothing can stop us, that there are no limitations on our creativity and resourcefulness.

The World often signifies wholeness that follows a period of intense personal or spiritual work. We comprehend and accept our place not only within our personal world, but within the greater community of all mankind as well. This is our integration with needs that reach beyond our personal goals.

Active in a relationship, it signals a time to celebrate joint attainments. It is the respite that follows completion and integration. We rejoice before we entertain thoughts of, or take steps toward, partaking in the next adventure or phase of our life and our relationship.

KEY WORDS AND PHRASES: freedom; completion; wholeness; movement; creativity; resourcefulness; perfection; new ventures; time to celebrate joint attainments; sexual fulfillment; no limitations.

_____
_____
_____
_____
_____

Chapter 4

Mundane Mysteries: Minor Arcana

The 56 Minor Arcana cards, with their four suits, later became the basis for the common playing cards used today. Traditionally, the suits symbolize the four elements of the world: air, earth, fire, water. In mystery schools those elements—and, by extrapolation, their suits—symbolized the four qualities of our psychic constitution: the mental or intellectual (air/Swords), the physical (earth/Pentacles), the spiritual (fire/Wands), and the emotional (water/Cups).[22]

In varying proportions, all things are comprised of the four elements, including our relationships. Some relationships have a predominance of or focus on one of the elements more than others.

Always on the go, the couple who frequently visit and travel have a predominance of Swords energy in their relationship. They are a bright couple who enjoy intellectual activities, seeking and clarifying the truth of issues, not only about their relationship, but about the world and their community.

The couple who are the salt of the earth and the backbone of their community have a Pentacles focus. They like to stay at home and value family togetherness, cozy conversations around the kitchen table. Service-oriented, they believe deeply in duty and in giving back to their community or their civic and professional organizations.

A couple with a Wands relationship are always interested in a variety of activities or issues and exude vitality. Whatever the activity—be it sexual, spiritual, or creative—they bring to it liveliness and a sense of the richness of life.

Couples whose focus is on Cups in its most positive sense are deeply involved with one another, showing concern for each other's feelings and for the well-being of others. However, since Cups is the element of emotions, a Cups relationship can also be one with a lot of intensity in the form of anger and resentment.

---

[22]Tony Willis, *Magick and the Tarot*, 1988.

Recognize yourself in one of those relationships? More likely, you discovered that aspects of all the elements are active in one or more of your relationships. Or one element is more predominant at times than others.

Minor Arcana cards, especially in the Rider-Waite deck, show facets of daily life, the "panorama of experience."[23]

In Tarot for Two readings we also use the card suits to show how people conceptualize and express themselves with respect to the issue, that is, objectively/logically (Swords), intuitively (Wands), emotionally (Cups), or practically (Pentacles).

In each suit there are four court cards—16 altogether—which show various characteristics of men and women. Having a number of court cards in a layout can indicate the many aspects of the self, that other people are involved, or that there are numerous outside influences on the situation.

Pages traditionally symbolize communication—input to the querent through conversation, telephone calls, letters, newspapers, magazines, and television. Qualities of flexibility, movement, youthfulness, and helpfulness are indicated by the Page cards. They can also represent either a young man or a young woman.

As warriors, the Knights symbolize strength, service, mobility, courage, victory with honor, and acting as champions for high ideals. Always ready to do battle with the forces to be overcome, Knights suggest action, sometimes hasty (Knight of Swords), which will need to be tempered with prudence or caution. Both women and men can make good use of the constructive forces symbolized by their Knight cards.

The Queens sit upon their thrones of authority, embodying the particular attribute of each suit in its highest feminine potential, available for the personal development of both men and women. Queen cards represent powers available for personal use and powers which can be delegated. They suggest inner serenity and the potential for integrating the various elements of the issue at hand.

Kings, as the archetype of masculine authority, not only carry out the laws but can remake them. King cards embody the qualities of initiative and willpower, whether for men or for women. Kings convey strong belief in one's principles and the potential for implementing them.

In addition to these traditionally determined qualities, we find it

---

[23]Rachel Pollack, *Seventy-Eight Degrees of Wisdom. Part 2: The Minor Arcana and Readings*, 1983, p. 8.

helpful for understanding relationship issues to regard the court cards as showing a progression of personal development.

Pages represent a somewhat immature approach to the present problem. When you draw a Page, it signals you need additional information to understand your responsibility in working toward solutions. Knights represent people who have achieved some degree of emotional maturity and experience and are able to put this know-how into action.

Queens and Kings have achieved self-mastery. They are in sufficient control of themselves to be able to assume or delegate responsibility.

So while we assume the Page role to tell you about the meanings of the Minor Arcana cards, we ask you to awaken your Knightly courage to charge through this aspect of your learning. We'll meet at the end of the chapter as accomplished Queens and Kings.

Wands: Budding Intuition

Commonly accepted understandings of the suit of Wands (also called staves or rods) include: ideas, intuition, inspiration, growth, renewal, passion, initiative, ambition, enterprise, enthusiasm.

All the Rider-Waite Wands have living leaves on them, suggesting the cyclic quality of the suit's attributes and also that Wands represents life and animation,[24] the creative force.

Representing the element of fire, Wands is considered a masculine suit.

---

[24]Arthur E. Waite, *The Pictorial Key to the Tarot*, 1971.

ACE OF WANDS

As with all aces, the Ace of Wands represents our access to the primordial energy of the suit and is clearly a gift from the higher powers (God, the forces of the universe, the cosmos—however you conceptualize your deities).

Because this suit is one of energy and creativity, the gift here is that of being alive. The leaves exploding off the bough in this card suggest more abundance in your life, relationships, or projects.

The Ace of Wands also denotes that you may receive the gift of an idea, possibly related to a new beginning, a novel enterprise, or a fresh, more lively direction in your relationship. It may represent the initiative or starting thrust you need to get going. Here is the energy, inspiration, and creative ability to make a relationship—the idea, and challenge, of how to grow together as one.

Sexually, the Ace of Wands represents masculine sexual initiative, sexual imagination, and the promise of sexual fulfillment.

KEY WORDS AND PHRASES: gift of an idea; creativity; new beginnings; initiative; starting thrust; enterprise; intuition; spiritual roots; sharing ideas; sexual imagination; promise of sexual fulfillment; masculine sexual initiative.

_____

_____

_____

_____

_____

TWO OF WANDS

Twos speak of choices, balance, and the struggle to achieve that. The Two of Wands, then, stresses our search for choice and balance in opportunities or ideas. When you draw this card, it may signify that to achieve balance, you and your other need to explore the issue at hand more actively.

From our two separate ways and experiences, we choose one path to follow for our relationship. Have the courage to see the "truth" as it is for you. Add the passions (red roses of desire) so dear to you in order to create or discover your own world together.

Depending on the heartprint where the Two of Wands appears, it can indicate we have a choice to make in the relationship, that we have two differing ideas, that new ideas will become available for us, or even that a world of ideas beckons to us. In other words, it is not the time to turn our backs on ideas, but rather to embrace them, explore them, and welcome the opportunity to make choices.

KEY WORDS AND PHRASES: choices; balance; discovery; questioning; two ideas; dominion; courage; achievement; the world beckons; exploring together; a world of sexual choices.

_____

_____

_____

_____

_____

THREE OF WANDS

As we engage in our relationships and their special qualities, our friends have different goals, wants, and drives. Their accomplishments do not diminish ours. We grow at our own pace and go where we need to go, stable within ourselves and within our relationships.

All threes have at their core our human dilemma between ideals and what we have to do to live in the real world. Drawing this card can mean that either you are already clear about your relationship commitment, or you are pondering your position in the relationship to decide exactly what your commitment will be.

The Three of Wands also indicates change in the sense that while we remain the same person or retain the same identity, we also change within that personality. This card reminds us that we are not our personalities, our ego, but rather, something larger. Trust, or get more in touch with, your intuitive processes, inner guides, or higher energies.

KEY WORDS AND PHRASES: stability; commitment; contemplation; three ideas; cooperation; movement; energetic interaction; expanding relationship horizons; sexual discovery; sexual satisfaction.

FOUR OF WANDS

Fours signal both the plateau that comes after the fruition of threes and the beginning of the energy buildup that propels us toward the next hurdle.

The Four of Wands reminds us that, in between the struggles of making a relationship work, it is important to take time to celebrate our accomplishments and triumphs. This is a card of recovery, of regaining strength to take the next step. It is also the time when we rededicate ourselves to the mutual enjoyment and happiness our relationships can bring.

During your Four of Wands respite, you may need to discover the fun of work or the fun in your work so you survive the next cycle less depleted.

KEY WORDS AND PHRASES: celebration; joy; prosperity; balance; four ideas; dedication; domestic harmony; mutual enjoyment; sexual celebration; fertile foundation.

_____
_____
_____
_____
_____

FIVE OF WANDS

Time to compare and share ideas. Fives usually involve a test of some kind, a struggle. The active construction and balance called for in a relationship expands our abilities and teaches us how to cooperate and to produce. But there may be disorganization as you wrestle with your ideas.

Which of the people in the card do you think you are, and what is your role in this group?

At its best, this card refers to the stimulation of ideas that occurs from the challenge of competition. Or it can mean it is time to examine your attitudes toward competition and modify them.

One understanding of the Five of Wands is that the people in the card are working together to create a star, a symbol of power. So the card is understood to reflect the power of working together.

Drawing this card signals that you or your relationship will experience heightened activity. Several relationships, or projects within a relationship, may compete for your time, and you may have to set priorities. Personally, you may experience this as a time of inner chaos as you wrestle with your own ideas.

KEY WORDS AND PHRASES: cooperation; comradeship; sharing; communication; comparing; balancing; establishing priorities; five ideas; competition; struggle; sexual competition; sexual bragging; attending to others' ideas about sex.

_____

_____

_____

_____

_____

SIX OF WANDS

Each success in a relationship gives us wisdom to draw upon and take into other relationships. Our persistent efforts will be rewarded. Six of Wands is victorious potential.

All sixes express reconciliation and advancement of the suit qualities. You can count on people outside the relationship to support your efforts or to have already supported your work and ideas. It is a good time to review your accomplishments. While you may be proud of them, be sure to acknowledge the efforts of others as well.

Although this card represents a real personal victory of which you can be proud, its negative aspect is that you have the potential for remaining too long on your "high horse," looking down on others. The positive aspect is that you have the vision to see what others cannot because they are too bogged down in mundane activities.

KEY WORDS AND PHRASES: victory; rewards; acknowledgment; six ideas or alternatives; validation; pride; accomplishments; sexual achievement; victory over inhibitions.

_____

_____

_____

_____

_____

SEVEN OF WANDS

Even though seven is a number of victory, the Minor Arcana sevens remind us of the variety of ways that success can be short-lived and challenged.

The Seven of Wands portrays those times when we must be well grounded and willing to hold our position in order to maintain what we believe in or what we have accomplished.

Drawing this card directs you to clarify your purposes in the relationships or the issue at hand. It can mean you already have the advantage, or that you need to use all your skills and powers to gain the advantage. Are you willing to defend your idea even if it is not a popular one? Or is it time to negotiate a mutual settlement?

KEY WORDS AND PHRASES: purpose; strength against adversity; building; gaining advantage; negotiation; seven ideas or alternatives; struggle; struggling with sexual identity; contending with past sexual ideas.

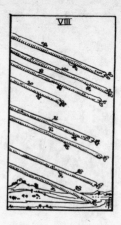

EIGHT OF WANDS

In a relationship, choices are the basis for growth, progress, and movement. Things are up in the air now, as yet undecided in your relationship. With respect to events already begun, choices await.

Eights remind us to reorder priorities, to reevaluate decisions, to take stock and reorganize.

What role will you choose to play in influencing the course of events—that of waiting patiently to see how things go, that of rushing ahead without careful deliberation, or that of taking some action that can change the course of events?

An explosion of ideas can seem overwhelming at first. Regard them as resources to help you make a choice.

KEY WORDS AND PHRASES: up in the air; movement; rushing ahead of deliberation; options; growth; eight ideas; sexual ideals.

_____

_____

_____

_____

_____

NINE OF WANDS

Your relationship has weathered the ego battles of the two of you. You have been resourceful in making it work. Having accomplished much, you are prepared, or preparing, to do the next thing that needs doing.

Nines illustrate completion, fulfillment, attainment, albeit not without wounds, as in the Nine of Wands.

In developing your strengths, you also have gained wisdom and experience, and it has been worth the effort. At the same time, you are cautious and alert about when and where the next challenge will arise. This may be an "attack" which never comes, so check whether you are expending too much energy in your defensive stance.

The wounded person in the card is looking toward the left edge of the card, the symbolic past. When you draw this card, it could indicate you are carrying problems from a past relationship into your present relationship. It might also signify difficulties in the present relationship due to past abuse either in adult relationships or in parent-child relationships.

KEY WORDS AND PHRASES: preparedness; awareness; resourcefulness; caution; waiting; deciding; defensive; nine ideas; sharing hurts; weighing sexual experiences; effects of the past.

_____

_____

_____

_____

_____

TEN OF WANDS

You have brought and continue to bring many ideas to your relationships. You may be so enamored with your viewpoint, however, that you are unable to see the value of others' ideas and suggestions. Your perspective is blocked.

This card asks you to consider expanding your horizon. Take another look at how far you have come in your relationship or how close you are to achieving your goals. You may be farther along than you think.

Whatever the load you are trying to carry alone, now may be the time to seek others' help or advice and not continue obstinately to persevere on your own.

You may be holding onto past sexual experiences and allowing your attitude or memories to shape your present sexual relationship, which may result in frustration for you or your mate.

Your determination and hard work will pay off because you have laid the foundation for the next step in your journey.

Tens illustrate endings and beginnings anew. Sometimes this feels like a definite burden ("not again"), but frequently, previous knowledge prevents you from making the same mistake twice. So while tens represent culmination, recommitment, and consolidation of your skills, ideas, wealth, etc., they also typify perseverance, in its best and worst sense.

KEY WORDS AND PHRASES: burden of success; oppressive load; fortitude; determination; foundation for next cycle; ten ideas; holding onto sexual experiences; sexual possessiveness.

PAGE OF WANDS

Based on your hard work and past efforts, you have a new idea, new insight into your relationship, or your relationship is taking a new direction or focus.

Drawing this card indicates receptivity to fresh ideas and input from others. You have started projects in the past that you have not finished. You may be distracted this time also and tempted to drop the ball. But it is time for you to commit and carry out your share in working on the relationship or the issue so that you may actually achieve the potential this card promises.

KEY WORDS AND PHRASES: messenger; new element in relationship; focus on central idea; new insight; open to input; necessary to carry one's load in the relationship.

_____
_____
_____
_____
_____

KNIGHT OF WANDS

Let's get busy; let's do something, anything. You have a lot of pent-up energy or excitement about your project or relationship, and you are ready to take action. But you may be ignoring ambivalent feelings you have about the issue.

It takes power, drive, and determination to accomplish what we want. Do you have the patience to see this project or issue to its conclusion?

If this is a sexual relationship and you are considering permanence, you may need to slow down. On the other hand, this card can signal that this is a sexual affair without care or commitment. It can be exciting, but don't be surprised if it doesn't last too long or if the sexual attraction fades as fast as it began.

KEY WORDS AND PHRASES: impetuous action; impatience; changes; departure; the idea of action; new outlook regarding sex; ideas for action; sexual dalliance; acting out sexual impulses.

_____

_____

_____

_____

_____

QUEEN OF WANDS

Now you are approaching the relationship or issue from a stable, creative perspective. You have been successful in the past and will, no doubt, apply that outlook to the present relationship or issue.

At least one of your relationships serves as a base of security from which you act with courage and authority. It fosters both your individuality and your creativity. You are comfortable with this project or relationship and have experienced (or will experience, depending on the heartprint) joy and growth out of it.

If you are a woman, you have achieved, or are well into the process of achieving, sexual maturity and are secure in your sexual needs and abilities. If you are a man, the feminine aspect of your personality is well developed and a source of inspiration for you to draw upon.

KEY WORDS AND PHRASES: creativity; energetic; successful; openness; encouraging; magnetic; leader; feminine viewpoint; feeling secure in sexual skills; sexual fertility; comfortable with sexual choices; sexually accomplished.

_____

_____

_____

_____

_____

KING OF WANDS

Yours is a tale of perseverance and success, based on traditional values. Relationships have grown and prospered as a result of your adventures and accomplishments.

You've learned from your mistakes and gained new abilities. Although you now have a rich background of skills and knowledge to draw upon for the future, you are not arrogant. Rather, you are able to view yourself from the perspective of one who is a relatively small cog in a larger picture. You may be quite spiritual in nature and see yourself in partnership with your deity or as having a rather humble but meaningful place in the universe.

If you are a man, you have achieved sexual maturity and are secure in your sexual needs and prowess. If you are a woman, the masculine aspect of your personality is available as an active resource from which to draw insight.

KEYWORDS AND PHRASES: benevolent authority; power; honesty; tradition; vitality; conscientious; tension; masculine viewpoint; doing one's best sexually; keeping a rein ("reign") on sexuality.

_____
_____
_____
_____
_____

Cups: Chalices of Emotion

The suit of Cups (sometimes referred to as chalices) represents human emotions and feelings, romance, the power of love, sensuality, creative and artistic expression, choices, and the plans which may develop from any of these. The downside of the suit for some is that it represents *all* emotions, including anger, hate, and fear. A feminine suit, Cups symbolizes the element of water.

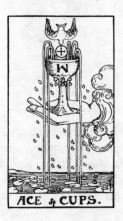

ACE OF CUPS

This is your chance for a new beginning within the early stages of romance, love, intense feelings, or passion. New aspects can now add to your relationship, such as exploring unique plans and expressing or clarifying your feelings and needs. Now is a good time to get in touch with, or to renew, the spiritual aspect of your relationship.

The droplets in the shape of Yods represent the most mystical and important letter of the Hebrew alphabet. They remind us to draw upon divine creative energy rather than our own egos. Then, truly, your "cup runneth over."

Use or explore the feminine aspects of yourself and trust those ideas. Another gift in the wings is the possibility of enriched sexual fulfillment through awakened senses and sensitivity.

KEYWORDS AND PHRASES: beginning stages of . . . (romance, love, etc.); joy; new aspect of relationship; intense feeling; nurturing; spiritual blessings; fully feminine; gift of a plan or direction; overflowing; intense sexual desire; promise of sexual satisfaction.

TWO OF CUPS

Your relationship is in (or will achieve, depending on card location) a state of harmony, for this is a card of cooperation. In part your search for harmony involves each of you finding your own space in the relationship and honoring and accepting your separate and special roles. Neither overwhelms the other.

The Two of Cups may relate to a specific, personal marriage, or it may refer to "marriage" in its broadest sense: as the alchemy of merging and balancing, working together to provide a new level of understanding. The two of you can come together in a way that will be healing and nourishing for both.

KEY WORDS AND PHRASES: relationship; romantic response; love; sensitivity; friendship; partnership; sexual dialogue; two plans or the plans of two; cooperation; harmony; sexual attraction; marriage; sexually balanced relationship; gentle masculine assertion.

_____

_____

_____

_____

THREE OF CUPS

Rejoice in your growth and victories and experience the healing of being happy together. Now is an appropriate opportunity for you to create a way of sharing your joy and abundance. Consider adding some special celebration rituals to your relationship.

If you have been working too hard, this card may be a reminder to take stock, but in a joyful, playful way. Remember, celebrations don't necessarily have to come at the end of hard work. They also can be a way of enhancing creativity prior to engaging in a new project.

KEY WORDS AND PHRASES: celebration; happiness; fulfillment; abundance; healing; sharing; emotional growth; three plans; sensuality; sexual sharing; sexual enjoyment; fertility.

_____
_____
_____
_____
_____

FOUR OF CUPS

This card can signal either the path of withdrawal and meditation for enlightenment and healing, or the path of defensiveness.

Knowing what you want is the first step in getting it. Review and consider your values and goals. Feelings of doubt and hesitancy are signs from our inner self that there is something to examine and evaluate. Having patience with ourselves and others gives us time to contemplate alternatives and choices. You may need to consider who or what is tempting you.

This card can also pinpoint a lethargic state that keeps you from interacting, or it can signal that you are too wounded or too defensive to consider another's proposal right now.

KEY WORDS AND PHRASES: reconsidering values; doubt; hesitancy; another choice; patience; introspection; contemplation; four plans; sexual dilemma; sexual withholding; not sexually adventurous.

_____

_____

_____

_____

_____

FIVE OF CUPS

Loss and change are part of the human condition. It may be time for you to grieve, or perhaps you have been disregarding something that you should have grieved about. Allow yourself that opportunity.

On the other hand, we can be so focused on the *idea* of loss that we lose sight of how really significant, or relatively insignificant, our loss is. Even when we gain a new insight or attitude, it sometimes feels like a loss, especially when the old way has been with us for a long time.

If you store lost opportunities and unmet expectations, and turn to them with regret and self-recrimination, it may be time to clean your emotional house. Review your priorities; change your plans; take stock of the resources you have left—or have been ignoring—that you can build on. Get back into the flow of your lifestream.

K E Y W O R D S A N D P H R A S E S : partial loss or change; unmet expectations; emotional confusion; change in priorities; concern; regrets over lost opportunities; choices; changing plans; taking stock.

_____

_____

_____

_____

_____

SIX OF CUPS

Sixes are cards of union and fulfillment, so the Six of Cups suggests a time of abundance and flowering in your relationship.

Let this card remind you to review how your relationships have enriched you and to relish those gifts. If you have not acknowledged that recently, let your mate or partner know. On the other hand, you may be ignoring skills which you developed from other relationships and which you could use in your present relationship.

If you have unfinished business from the past that is negatively influencing present relationships, consider its place in your life—perhaps the lessons you've learned—and then put it to rest.

According to the late psychiatrist Eric Berne,[25] the child ego state is the source of our playful attitudes and of joyful sex. In your personal relationship, it is time to attend to and acknowledge your inner child.

KEY WORDS AND PHRASES: gifts; care; childhood memories; reflections on youth; concern for family; reconciliation; harmony; nostalgia; playfulness; sexual opportunity; childhood sexual feelings; nostalgia for past relationships.

_____
_____
_____
_____
_____

---

[25]Founder of Transactional Analysis and author of *Games People Play*, 1964.

SEVEN OF CUPS

You are actively fantasizing or dreaming about the kind of choices that will enrich your life and your relationships.

An essential component of hope is the belief that we have, and can make, choices. That is the positive aspect of the Seven of Cups.

Consider the role of hope in your relationship or issue question. Do you need more hope, more belief in your ability to make choices? Or are you hoping unrealistically when you should be taking action or establishing priorities so you will not be overwhelmed?

In its negative aspect this card suggests that your dreams are in the clouds and the promised "wealth" of a relationship is illusory. Take care that you are not overestimating the mental and physical riches a potential partner might bring into the relationship, either by projecting onto him or her the riches you have to offer or by not attending to all the signals you are receiving.

KEY WORDS AND PHRASES: abundant choices; needing to choose; imagination; daydreams; being overwhelmed; abundance of desires; confusion; sexual fantasies.

_____
_____
_____
_____
_____

EIGHT OF CUPS

The Eight of Cups signals a time of seeking and of transition, a time to consider changing direction or emphasis.

The figure is moving toward the mountain of higher truth, so you may need to commit to higher ideals rather than superficial values in your personal life or in your relationship. The Eight of Cups also can notify you to begin your personal journey toward the spiritual, or your exploration of your unconscious or inner workings.

This card raises the question of whether you should walk away from or let go of a relationship—present or past—that is completed, or that is destructive for you. Time to turn toward a new direction?

In its negative sense the card suggests a perfectionistic attitude: rejecting a person or project because you think it is flawed. Reevaluate from a broader or more spiritual perspective.

KEY WORDS AND PHRASES: change of direction; new beginnings; emotional reevaluation; detachment; shyness or withdrawal; commitment to higher values; sexual sublimation; exploring an alternative lifestyle; turning away from convention.

NINE OF CUPS

Material happiness and abundance, contentment and satisfaction, that's Nine of Cups time. Truly you have made your wishes come true. You can be proud of your hard work, which has finally paid off.

Drawing this card may also mean you have a number of new plans and ideas for your relationship or about the issue question.

The crossed arms of the figure caution you against basking in your success in such a way that you close yourself off to others or to the next stage of your experience.

KEY WORDS AND PHRASES: fulfillment; success; emotional contentment and security; wishes come true; pride; a variety of plans; good health; sexual satisfaction; sexual variety.

_____

_____

_____

_____

_____

TEN OF CUPS

Drawing the Ten of Cups signifies not only the physical but the emotional wealth that results from your relationship efforts, especially family endeavors. A high stage of fulfillment in your relationship, an achievement of harmony, are yours.

Take time now, before the new work begins—remember, tens signal fruitful completion prior to a new cycle—to acknowledge your own and the other's efforts and accomplishments.

With respect to inner or personal work, all aspects of yourself are integrated and functioning on a harmonious plane.

KEY WORDS AND PHRASES: emotional fulfillment; peaceful family life; harmony; promise of more to come; safe haven; completion of cycle; abundance; sexual commitment.

_____
_____
_____
_____

PAGE OF CUPS

Your emotional awareness has reached a new level of sensitivity, or you have achieved a new level of emotional security in your relationship. You are conscious of present and past cycles and can use that knowledge in planning.

Since you have prepared yourself, now is a good time to focus on one specific emotional aspect of your relationship or issue. At this time you will be less distracted in your relationship work or in projects.

KEY WORDS AND PHRASES: creativity; consciousness; imagination taking form; increased awareness; emotional sensitivity; sensitive, imaginative lover; new conquests.

_____

_____

_____

_____

_____

KNIGHT OF CUPS

Having completed your deliberations, you are on the verge of setting out on your quest. Presently poised on the brink of a relationship or project, you are well prepared and sufficiently secure emotionally to make the journey.

Whether you are a male playing the role of "knight in shining armor" or a female with a new knight, take care to explore the level of facade and the level of genuineness in your roles. Check out your dreams.

If you are ready to go dashing off and rescue someone, think twice about whether or not that person really wants to be rescued. This card alerts you to evaluate the quantity and quality of your rescuing activities.
KEY WORDS AND PHRASES: practical plan; opportunity or invitation to love; emotional intensity; "knight in shining armor"; persistent courting; acting out emotions.

QUEEN OF CUPS

Emotions play a high priority in your life. You may be experiencing a lot of emotional intensity in your projects and relationships, especially family ones. Either they are at a new pitch or you have a more intense involvement.

The emotional complexities of past relationships or activities have become clear to you. In present relationships or projects you will be the one who directs the focus toward their emotional aspects. This is a time of imaginative creativity for you as you allow your emotions to inspire you. Your experience will be respected and your contributions valued.

KEYWORDS AND PHRASES: focused; imaginative; emotionally responsive; sensitivity; empathy; strength; maternal; sexual display; flamboyant sex; sexual intensity.

_____
_____
_____
_____
_____

KING OF CUPS

If you can remain levelheaded when all about you others are in turmoil, you are the King of Cups.

Drawing this card indicates that a new, stabilizing force has entered your life or your projects, or that you have reached a new level of emotional stability and maturity.

Well satisfied with your emotional examination of the question or issue, you can act creatively and from emotional security. However, you do this with discipline rather than on impulse. You are also quite capable, and often put aside your personal needs—or suppress your emotions—to help others, especially your professional or social community.

When you have reached this pinnacle in your relationship, you are well able to evaluate the roles played by your own emotions and those of others, and to make a capable decision taking these aspects into account. In all situations you keep your perspective, able to laugh at your own foibles and those of others. You come across as a human leader who inspires devotion, because you allow others to see your humanity.

KEY WORDS AND PHRASES: stability; worldliness; creativity; kindliness; generosity; leader; wise; supportive; working behind the scenes; sexual integration.

_____

_____

_____

_____

_____

Swords: Cutting Through Illusion

Swords traditionally is interpreted as a suit of bleak, desolate cards, indicating violent or negative actions and emotions portending disaster.

For years we have attended workshops where leaders promised to give us more positive definitions of Swords and didn't.

Kaplan's idea that a suit sequence might present a story inspired us to examine Swords more carefully. Our studies with teachers of the esoteric led us to regard Swords as actually having an esoteric, or hidden, meaning, often the reverse of the apparent meaning.

Attention to *all* the symbols on the cards reveals Swords as the suit which foretells the intuitive development awaiting us when logic and reason—and the illusion of rationality—have failed. If we give up the myth that we can resolve all our mundane issues through logic and rationality, we make room for the wisdom of the heart.

But, as the Swords suggests, many of us must face great personal battles before we are ready or willing to give up objectivity as the single best way to resolve issues. The battle, or journey, is not one of simply learning to be more emotional. It also includes learning, trusting, and drawing upon "the coding of all our becomings,"[26] our human heritage.

In more traditional approaches, Swords symbolizes discrimination, action, competition, conflict, basic skills of craftsmanship, or survival. They may indicate the imminence of legal matters, written contracts, verbal disputes, as well as the ability to make decisions or "cut through illusions." Possessing the inner abilities necessary to make the spiritual quest is another Swords characteristic.

All the swords depicted in the Rider-Waite deck are double-edged, often bringing relief by cutting away the excessive or unnecessary. Depending on how they are influenced by the other cards in the spread, they may be interpreted as constructive or destructive. They represent the element of air and are a masculine suit.

---

[26]Jean Houston, *Lifeforce: The Psycho-Historical Recovery of the Self,* 1980, p. 3.

ACE OF SWORDS

With the Ace of Swords we receive the gift of our birthright: the ability to combine logic and intuition to achieve clarity. Below us, the jagged brown-and-blue mountains suggest we will successfully achieve balance in our relationships between the worldly and the intuitive, but not without a struggle. This card of new beginning recognizes the need for balance before the work has begun.

Have the courage to challenge the routines, the set roles, or the rules, in whatever form they appear, in your project or relationship. Victory will be yours, but first you may have to sacrifice your egotistical viewpoint.

The Ace of Swords also indicates that there is a wise and benevolent authority whom you would do well to consult for additional information. **KEY WORDS AND PHRASES**: gift of an ability; rational skills; new concept; power; virtue; talent; force; conquest; potential for sexual fulfillment; sexual power; joining forces.

_____

_____

_____

_____

_____

TWO OF SWORDS

At its simplest, the Two of Swords reflects your reluctance to face something in your life or in the relationship issue.

Closed off to your heart's reason and your inner wisdom, you are unwilling to acknowledge the role your intuitive, subjective processes can play, or are playing. But your so-called rational approach is only a pose. You are in a standoff with yourself.

Consider that you may be falsely protecting against another's invasion where no threat exists.

This card also signals preparedness and patience. You sense, on an intuitive level, the need for balance and have the ability to be ready to use your talents.

KEY WORDS AND PHRASES: waiting; choice; compromise; stalemate; considering two answers; sexual resistance; sexual or emotional protection.

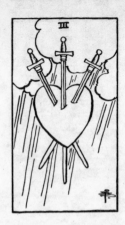

THREE OF SWORDS

One of the simplified, more traditional meanings of the Three of Swords is "heartbreak." Look again. In fact, the swords have penetrated a cartoon heart; there is no blood. The clouds, becoming lighter, indicate a change for the better. This is false heartbreak.

Drawing this card suggests that whatever the issue or question you are pondering, it is not a conflict of the heart. Look to other aspects, such as the environment, attitudes, or past conditioning.

The journey of integrating objective and subjective into your personal life or into the relationship issue has begun. It may be painful, but not fatal, and at this point you experience your first, small victory in the skirmishes to come.

This card sometimes signals that it is time in a relationship to acknowledge and experience your pain in an open, honest way, without manipulation.

KEY WORDS AND PHRASES: the three swords of logic, reason, and detachment pierce the emotions; holding back emotions; intellectual, emotional, or material loss; fear of grief; no blood drawn; "the heart of the problem"; sexual frustration.

_____

_____

_____

_____

_____

FOUR OF SWORDS

Time out for reverie. This card calls for the kind of meditation or introspection that permits you to integrate all that has been going on in your relationship. It can also identify your need to arrange for activities that heal you personally or are healing to the relationship.

Drawing the Four of Swords can signal that you are asleep to possibilities within the relationship or to the intervention of higher guidance.

It alludes to the wholeness we can experience when we integrate our intellect and our spirituality with our cultural rituals and mythology. You may need to make these more a part of your relationship, or to consider how they are affecting your relationship.

KEY WORDS AND PHRASES: rest; healing; meditation; introspection; retreat; solitude; redefining needs; turning inward; letting the issue rest; sexual sublimation; celibacy; conserving sexual energy.

_____

_____

_____

_____

_____

FIVE OF SWORDS

Not only can we learn from our own journey, but we can also learn from others, from their attitudes as well as their victories and defeats. Does someone have something to teach you now?

The Five of Swords can indicate your need to salvage what has been of value from past situations and bring that into the present.

In its negative sense this card is sometimes considered to indicate someone taking advantage of other people or situations. Is that a possibility in your present relationship or issue?

A present victory can have costly consequences for you, especially if you attempt to get it by manipulating or exploiting others. On the other hand, take care that you are not the exploited one.

KEY WORDS AND PHRASES: opportunist; taking advantage of existing situation; manipulation; conquest; maneuvering; exploiter; misuse of abilities; humiliating others; sexual conquest; lost sexual opportunities.

_____

_____

_____

_____

_____

SIX OF SWORDS

You have completed one phase of your growth, or of a project, and it is time to continue the journey, to take action once more. Another opportunity for change and transition. How will you face it?

If this is a personality or personal issue, several aspects of your personality are involved: certainly your anima (feminine), your animus (masculine), and your inner child. This is a passage you have to make, and while you may feel sad about it, or it may seem insurmountable at times, the promise of new and fertile growth lies ahead. You do have the strength to achieve your goal.

KEY WORDS AND PHRASES: choosing to change; change of mental state; intellectual development; increased understanding; harmony of values; elevation in consciousness; moving; journey; navigating a transition; limited sexual scope; changing sexual expression.

_____

_____

_____

_____

_____

SEVEN OF SWORDS

In its best sense, this is a card of mindlessness, of not being fully aware of the consequences of your actions. At its worst, it indicates deceit and betrayal. Consider whether you are trying to "get away with something" or whether someone is trying to take something from you without earning it.

Because the Seven of Swords signifies distraction from the real issue of the relationship or project, or a secret agenda, plans made at this time may ultimately fail. Take more time to consider; do not act hastily or impulsively.

KEY WORDS AND PHRASES: manipulation; deviousness; derring-do; coup d'état; impulsiveness; ingenious planning; completion of mental cycle; independent action; calculation; unwarranted secrecy; vigilance; sexual exploitation.

_____
_____
_____
_____
_____

EIGHT OF SWORDS

The bad news is that the Eight of Swords speaks of being blinded and trapped. The good news is that it is usually our own thinking or illusion that traps us.

When you draw this card, raise the issue of whether or not you are operating on false assumptions or illusionary thinking that is blocking your progress. Check your premises, open your eyes, and question your own or another's viewpoint. There are more choices to be discovered.

Examine past incidents to determine whether they offer wisdom or insight about your present situation or whether they are the source of your entrapment. Do not be bound by the opinions of others.

KEY WORDS AND PHRASES: temporary helplessness; not seeing abilities; overlooking possibilities; indecision; restriction; domination; isolation; need for mental effort; sexual frustration; hindered by sexual attitudes.

_____
_____
_____
_____
_____

NINE OF SWORDS

When you draw this card, it may signify a time of separation or separateness in your relationship or your projects. Caught up in not seeing the broader perspective, you ignore a passionate or more worldly view. Personally, you may be disregarding the talents you bring to the relationship.

The Nine of Swords can also mean you have taken on the sorrows or worries of others and are now burdened with them, possibly overwhelmed. You cannot avoid your own problems by shifting to those of others, and you cannot solve theirs. Become selective about which sorrows you are going to attend to or allow to make a difference in your life or relationships.

If there is conflict in a relationship, you may have difficulty explaining your point of view or understanding the viewpoint of another.

This card sometimes indicates the emergence of deep, hidden shame which needs to be acknowledged and resolved. Some regard the figure on the card as in a state of depression. If that makes sense for your present state of being, you need to explore what angers or illusions may be immobilizing you. Sometimes the figure is seen as awakening from the logical approach and opening to the resources symbolized by the elements on the quilt and bed.

KEY WORDS AND PHRASES: self-appraisal; analyzing dreams; turning sorrow into possibilities; integrating experience into wisdom; introspection; reevaluation; need to refocus goals; sexual conflict; sexual nightmare; refusal to face sexuality.

TEN OF SWORDS

As all tens do, this card signifies an end and a new dawning. In this case, it is that end to illusion that must take place before your relationship, or you as an individual, can begin a higher, more enlightened level of functioning.

The Ten of Swords is one of the most powerful and complex cards in the deck. Drawing it raises the question of how your ego prevents or interferes with harmonious relationship decisions. You may have to give up some of your ideas or conditioning before you and the relationship can move to a new level of involvement.

The swords along the spine symbolize a new alignment with higher, possibly spiritual, energies.[27] This card also contains one of the most obvious mudras (finger positions) in the Rider-Waite deck. The thumb touches the ring finger in the Buddhist mudra of "kichijo-in," symbolizing good fortune or joy.[28]

In mudra theory, the five fingers of the hand represent chakras (energy centers). The ring finger represents the second chakra of decision. The thumb represents the fifth chakra of communication. The Ten of Swords mudra, then, identifies an individual in the process of signaling a conscious decision to evolve toward harmony.

---

[27]We thank Georgia Lambert R. for this insight.
[28]E. Dale Saunders, *Mudra. A Study of Symbolic Gestures in Japanese Buddhist Sculpture*, 1960.

KEY WORDS AND PHRASES: "dark night of the soul" before balancing the intuitive and emotional; release from obsession; discarding illusions; another approach needed; viewpoints being transformed; burdened by conditioning; end of strife.

PAGE OF SWORDS

Having rid yourself of the illusions that blinded or hindered you, you are ready for action. You are prepared and vigilant for what comes next, and it is coming. However, there is an unevenness to your relationships. You may want to spend some time identifying and analyzing that.

You have the confidence that comes from past experience and you do not need to be, nor will you be, defensive in your interactions. You come from a place of wisdom based on experience.

KEY WORDS AND PHRASES: poised for action; balanced approach involving physical and mental dexterity; vigilance; perception; investigation; sexual confidence; sexual competency.

KNIGHT OF SWORDS

This is the card of dramatically changing, but not necessarily of ending, your relationship. Time to recognize and confront destructive elements in your relationship. It is also a good time to reexamine, and possibly modify, your respective roles.

Impetuousness and impatience are at a high intensity now. Take care that you use your energy positively for analysis and planned change rather than reorganizing out of anxiety—what psychologists call "acting out."

Sometimes the knight on the card is seen as being threatened. Check whether someone or something is an active threat to your situation or position.

KEY WORDS AND PHRASES: impetuous; hasty; incisive mind; daring; champion; impatience; bravery; skill; destroying to create anew; sexual change or challenge; sexual tension.

_____

_____

_____

_____

_____

QUEEN OF SWORDS

Whether you are male or female, anytime you have finished grieving and have transformed the essence of your sorrow into wisdom, you have incorporated the major aspect of the Queen of Swords.

Drawing this card signals that you are suppressing or controlling your emotions in the service of a more intellectual position. Your thoughts are with projects for the future rather than dwelling on the past.

In its best sense, this is a time when you will compassionately review a problem or situation. Negatively, you may act very judgmentally. In either case, your position will be one of an outsider rather than a participant.

KEY WORDS AND PHRASES: strong character; authority; judging; suppressed emotions; logic tempered with wisdom; feminine reasoning; sexually on guard; sex on one's own terms.

_____
_____
_____
_____
_____

KING OF SWORDS

As the King of Swords, you acknowledge and face your relationships as they are. You are ready to act on what needs to be done for the sake of the relationship.

You may be entering a period when you will be your own best friend. Your ideas and emotions will entertain you more than those of others. If you are considering a new partner in any endeavor, take care to see to it that his or her capacities match your own, or you will soon find yourself bored.

Intuitive skills, tempered by the wisdom of intellect and emotional experience, are at their peak now. But your talisman sword reminds you that, separately, either intellectual reasoning or heart reasoning alone can only get you so far.

KEYWORDS AND PHRASES: authority; wisdom; patriarchal values; rule maker; action; aware; articulate; assertive; direct; prudent; capable; caring sexual partner; secure sexual identity; masculine reasoning.

_____
_____
_____
_____
_____

Pentacles: Coins of the Realm

Pentacles, called coins or disks in some decks, represents possessions, personal resources, business matters, ecological concerns, and material gain.

A suit of service, Pentacles shows how we use our physical abilities and talents for creation and accomplishment. It represents the actual manifestation, or production, of the qualities of the previous three suits: ideas (Wands), plans (Cups), and abilities (Swords).

In a spiritual sense, Pentacles suggests flexibility of the mind and the spirit. Representing the earth element, it is a female suit.

ACE OF PENTACLES

You are offered the ability to be in the present with clear, rather than obscured, vision or thought. Definite and focused about the tasks that need to be completed, you attend to them from a position of insight.

Now is a time when any "duties" required of you can be accomplished joyfully and easily. Working on projects or your relationship promises an abundant payoff materially, financially, or emotionally.

KEY WORDS AND PHRASES: gift of manifesting; power to accomplish; initiative; prosperity; physical and financial potential; starting a new path; promise of fertility; potential for abundance; shared values.

_____

_____

_____

_____

_____

TWO OF PENTACLES

Stay alert to things you will be called upon to balance. At one end of the continuum, it is possible that for a while you will feel temporarily off-balance. Your relationships may be a little topsy-turvy. On the other hand, you may be handling a couple of situations with real ease.

You have a seemingly infinite capacity now to put, or keep, things in balance, even though for a time you may feel you are juggling too many things at once. Do you need to rely on or allow another to help you gain your equilibrium or stability? Look for equality and sharing in your relationships and projects.

Emotionally, if you are a person who "keeps score" in your relationships, it is time to balance the books and develop a new way of being together.

KEY WORDS AND PHRASES: balancing; choices; adaptation to change; dexterity and agility in dealing with material things; balancing one another in the relationship; sexual performer; sexual agility.

_____
_____
_____
_____
_____

THREE OF PENTACLES

Teamwork and cooperation is one of the themes of this card. The structure of your joint relationship or project is sound. The details of how you work together on it need to be clarified.

Drawing this card can also indicate that you have mastered the skills you need and your inner triumvirate (body, mind, spirit) is working together to accomplish a current goal. Engaged in a process or project you totally love, you have no ambivalence.

This card also presents the message that work serves as your pathway for personal growth. Your participation in work completed, or about to be (depending on the heartprint)—or your attitude toward it—elevates you to a higher state of personal development.

KEY WORDS AND PHRASES: master builder; artist; craftsmanship; skilled labor; recognition of skills; supportive partners; knowledge; professional growth; spiritual growth through work or service; material gain; able to experience sex in a variety of aspects.

_____
_____
_____
_____
_____

FOUR OF PENTACLES

We can become so attached to our possessions or to acquiring wealth that we turn our backs on family and community service.

Negatively, the Four of Pentacles indicates an attitude of distrust and a need to hold onto what we have. Emotionally, this often relates to low self-esteem and the belief that no better project or relationship will come along. Any attitude you are "hanging onto" now offers only a false sense of security.

When you draw this card, it can also signify a lack of faith that you or your colleagues can straighten things out. Both your heart and your mind are closed to new input.

KEY WORDS AND PHRASES: holding onto possessions or beliefs; ownership; attachments; position and status; security; unwillingness to share; sexually self-focused.

_____
_____
_____
_____
_____

FIVE OF PENTACLES

Your perceptions of yourself as "wounded," mentally or emotionally impoverished, or unworthy limit your progress.

Drawing this card may signal that some social institution—your church, your family, a counseling center—could help you if you can see your way to allow this. Take care that false pride does not close off these opportunities to you.

Personally, this card can also indicate that you are in a codependent relationship, are being victimized by a relationship, or are simply feeling "out in the cold." Injuries you sustain now—whether physical or emotional, actual or illusional—can be used as a turning point (fives are the midpoint of the cycle) for better or for worse, depending on whether your thinking is clear or distorted.

KEY WORDS AND PHRASES: victim consciousness; need to overcome spiritual separation; overlooking possibilities for change; overemphasis on material/financial problems; not asking for help; confusion; soul-searching; sexual problems.

_____
_____
_____
_____
_____

SIX OF PENTACLES

This is another card which raises issues of balance in your life and your projects. It signals a time to evaluate how and where you are in balance and where your life or projects are out of balance.

Are you giving enough to yourself? Do you feel like you are being given scraps, or less than you should receive, financially or emotionally? Has something or someone been put on hold while you direct your attention to something else? Is there someone or something toward which you should be more generous?

When you draw this card, it can also signal a possible shift in power or authority which may not be all it seems.

If your issue is an individual or personal one, consider whether there is some aspect of yourself to which you are not giving enough attention.

KEY WORDS AND PHRASES: willingness to share; generosity; philanthropy; fairness; kindness; consideration; financial rewards; gifts; limited sexual giving.

_____
_____
_____
_____
_____

SEVEN OF PENTACLES

Although the rewards of our accomplishments are near, we are not finished yet. This card signals a time to take stock, perhaps a brief respite, but reminds us there is still more work to be done before our project or issue reaches fulfillment.

Persevere; success is at hand. Now is not the time to cancel or drop present projects or relationships. The potential for fruition is still to come.

You may be tempted to turn your attention to projects or relationships that appear to be more fruitful or rewarding. Take your time and lay the groundwork for any project or relationship you are considering or presently beginning.

KEYWORDS AND PHRASES: waiting for fruition; evaluating accomplishments; waiting patiently; daydreaming; sexual accomplishment.

_____

_____

_____

_____

_____

EIGHT OF PENTACLES

Your skills are well developed. You are a producer and you know it. When you are given a task or accept one, you will accomplish it. Your output can be relied on. Training and perseverance pay off at last.

On the one hand, this card suggests you have reached a level of proficiency where work or interaction has become easy for you. On the other hand, you could be reaching a stage where your work or relationship is becoming repetitive and boring. Vary your activities to add a new dimension and to avoid boredom in your relationship or burnout at work.

Another aspect of this card is the necessity for discipline and training. You may need to update the talents that enhance your work or home relationship skills. Consider the possibility of learning new techniques.

The Eight of Pentacles sometimes indicates too much focus on your work and not enough attention to other relationships.

KEY WORDS AND PHRASES: growth and accomplishment through work; acceptance of responsibility; patient effort; learning new skills; apprenticeship; production; willingness to learn new sexual skills; patience with a partner.

_____
_____
_____
_____
_____

NINE OF PENTACLES

As a result of your efforts, abundance is yours. You now relish and appreciate the fruits of your labors. This card reminds us both to take time to enjoy and to continue or begin anew at our own pace.

Drawing the Nine of Pentacles indicates financial or emotional success that comes about through a high level of accomplishment. This is a time in your relationship or project when your self-reliance is at its peak. Because you are so confident and satisfied, you may have a tendency to rely too much on yourself and be a little too independent or aloof.

If you are a man, this card signals you may now successfully draw upon the feminine side of your personality or wisdom to aid you in your accomplishments.

KEY WORDS AND PHRASES: enjoying accomplishments; prosperity; financial stability; abundance; independence; access to natural resources; sexual satisfaction; enjoying sexual achievement.

_____

_____

_____

_____

_____

TEN OF PENTACLES

The Ten of Pentacles is another complex and powerful card. Commonly understood as a card of material and familial prosperity, it is much more.

The pentacles take the form of the cabalistic Tree of Life, a specific pattern depicting the ten qualities of God's powers and the inner foundation of every human. So this card addresses "higher" issues, the achievement of an emotional or spiritual prosperity.

We have earned and taken our rightful place as part of a family and a community. We honor our traditional heritage. We recognize and accept our place in a spiritual community.

If your issue is a personal one, this card signals the ending of a fruitful phase of work on yourself as preparation for the beginning of a new phase of great spiritual or enlightened growth.

KEY WORDS AND PHRASES: family relationships; home; cultural values and traditions; wealth; family heritage, prosperity and teachings; fullness of life; security; traditional sexual values.

_____
_____
_____
_____
_____

PAGE OF PENTACLES

Evaluate your relationship or project, not for past achievements, but rather with an eye toward what can still be accomplished. Focus your efforts on planning now. You may be considering involvement in a fascinating new project or interest.

At this time you see the true value for you of your relationship, rather than for any truths or ideals advocated by others.

Self-involved now, you want and like what *you* want and like. Others' interests are less important to you. The downside of this attribute is that you can become so focused on pursuing your own interests that you are insensitive to the needs of others.

KEY WORDS AND PHRASES: diligence in study and work; technician; planner; foreman; resourceful; concentration; sexual student.

KNIGHT OF PENTACLES

Although you claim to be willing to work on a project or relationship, you also don't want to be affected by it. You put in your time—or even more than is expected of you—but it is effort without any passion because you won't allow it to touch you, or because you have lost it.

You have a tendency to get things done and be through with them—perhaps perpetually putting off your own pleasure for the sake of the project or others. This card calls for you to renew and awaken your own dormant passions.

KEY WORDS AND PHRASES: overseer; hard worker; materialistic; responsible; persistent; principled; stable; practical; defender of traditional values; sexual endurance; slow but deep development of love; faithfulness.

_____
_____
_____
_____
_____

QUEEN of PENTACLES

QUEEN OF PENTACLES

The Queen of Pentacles represents not just dedication, but the kind of devotion to projects or relationships that pays off, frequently more for others than for ourselves. When you draw this card, you are clear about the nature of your relationships. Your efforts will unify everyone involved.

To others your energy appears boundless. You truly serve with love and love your service. The downside of this attribute is that we take our queens for granted and seldom give them the accolades they deserve.

In its negative aspect, the Queen of Pentacles signals that your social values or service outweighs your personal or family needs. You may need to reorder your priorities.

KEY WORDS AND PHRASES: at home in the world; self-trust; opulence; authority; security; sensuous; thoughtful; dependable; generous; fruitful efforts; earth mother; feminine accomplishments.

_____

_____

_____

_____

_____

KING of PENTACLES.

KING OF PENTACLES

Your appearance and possessions show you have succeeded. You toiled for it and you intend to enjoy it.

At its best, this card can indicate a steady, reliable partner, generous and considerate of the needs of others. You act quickly on your well-honed skill in identifying what will or won't work.

The downside of this card, however, is that you may be so stubbornly involved with your business efforts that family or personal relationships suffer.

KEY WORDS AND PHRASES: strong, forceful character; the sweet life; intelligent; savvy; materialistic; accomplished; realistic; practical; stable; business leader; mathematical and financial aptitude; confident sexual identity; sexually mature.

_____

_____

_____

_____

_____

Chapter 5

Refining the Likeness

Remember when you first learned to drive? How frustrating it was to stay abreast of the traffic around (where did it all come from?) while trying to keep the car headed straight, figure out how and when to signal, check the rearview mirror, and watch for changing lights.

Like us, you must have wondered if you would ever be able to release your death grip on the wheel or when you would be able to stop holding your breath and begin holding a conversation.

That same sense of being overwhelmed is common when you begin learning to read the Tarot cards or to make sense out of a Tarot for Two spread. As cards are turned over, you must elicit appropriate information from each, compare the two cards in each heartprint, put all this together to relate to your question, and carry on a dialogue with your partner—or the person you are reading for, if you are reading for someone else. At first it may seem almost as unmanageable as your maiden moment behind that wheel.

However, if you take it one step at a time, then each element on the card, each single card, and, finally, each pair of cards make sense.

Concentrate first on understanding the meaning of the card and how that meaning changes slightly, depending on the heartprint. You are learning what your brushes (cards) can do and the principles of artistic construction (heartprints).

As you become more accomplished, you can refine your understanding even more by attending to the various symbols—we call them heart codes—from Chapter 8. They enhance your artistic style and flair.

Use the following refining guidelines to help you make sense of the elements and symbols on each pair of cards. Why not pick two cards from your own deck to look at as you read the guidelines?

When you lay down cards for the Tarot for Two spread, consider:

1. The activities occurring in each of the two cards and whether they complement or hinder each other.
2. The elements on the cards which seem to jump out at you as relevant to the question and the situation.

3. The predominant colors and what information they may offer in relation to the question (see Chapter 8).
4. How the numerical value of the card or the number of objects on the card relates to the question (see Chapter 8).
5. Whether the predominant mood, the weather, or the time of day indicated is significant to the question.
6. What sexual interactions or implications are shown by the cards.
7. Whether astrological compatibilities are shown by the cards (see Chapter 8).

In the beginning, make a note of your reactions so you can check them out with the symbolic meanings for colors, numbers, and objects in Chapter 8. As you become more familiar with symbology, more ideas will come to you.

Don't worry about getting the significance of all the elements on the card. Learning Tarot heart codes is a little like learning a foreign language. If you take one word at a time to begin with, soon you will be putting together sentences.

Attend to those symbols that strike you first. That's your unconscious signaling you. Sometimes the symbolic message is readily apparent. Sometimes you hold the message-possibility in your mind, or on your notepad, as something you need to check or clarify as additional cards are turned up.

To practice looking for the points above, do the following exercise:

Exercise 5—Answering Refining Guideline Questions for Two Cards:
One of your female friends has learned that you can read the Tarot for Two. She asks you, "How can I enhance my sexual relationship with my lover?"

Shuffle your cards, concentrating on her question. Draw any two cards from your deck. Designate one to represent your friend and one to represent her lover. Do not be concerned about the heartprint at this time.

Using the card meanings and the guidelines in this chapter, compare the information obtainable from the two cards. What have you learned about these two people?

When one of our students did this exercise, she drew the Knight of Pentacles for the woman and The Devil (Major Arcana XV) for the man. Take a look at these cards from your own deck. What do they tell you? Make a few notes before you compare your thoughts with those of our student.

Here's how she made sense of the cards. First from the card meanings: the woman will do whatever she or they decide—she will put in the effort—but without a lot of passion. Although she may need to be the force that keeps this issue alive (the work of Pentacles, the hidden aspect of The Devil card), she also needs to find some way to revive her passion for the relationship. He has some false ideas about their relationship which need to be acknowledged and overcome. That exploration may bring new life into the relationship and revive the passions of both.

Next our student added to that information by following the refining guidelines: there doesn't seem to be a whole lot of action taking place for either of them at this time. Perhaps the question arises out of this stalemate. She is approaching the issue from an intellectual perspective (yellow background) as if willpower will resolve the issue; however, that will not help until he is willing to attend to the power of whatever is presently hidden (blocked?) from his awareness (black background).

She sits on her intuition or instincts and needs to spur them into action (horse). He, too, is restrained (chains). The potential for success (more excitement?) is there for her (the numerological aspects of 12; also $2 + 1 = 3$), although he is likely to benefit more from their working on this issue (15; also $5 + 1 = 6$).

What else were you able to ascertain from the cards? If you have not done so already, you now might like to draw your own pair of cards and complete Exercise 5.

Part 3

Tarot Tips

Tarot Tutor 3

When we visit another culture or country and observe a folk performance, most of us don't think twice about what went beforehand. We just enjoy.

But for many of the tribal, cultural, or aboriginal arts, specific ceremonial preparations occur before the performance ever begins. More than just the readying of costumes or the applying of makeup or masks, significant prayers or rituals are crucial to the success of the performance, which is intended in some way to revive and restore community or universal harmony. The ultimate performance might even be said to begin with those rituals.

We consider a Tarot for Two reading as the unfoldment of a microcosmic drama, with components similar to many restorative folk ceremonies that still survive in other cultures. Although Part 3 reviews what may appear to some as elementary how-tos, in fact what we're really asking you to do *is* think twice about your preparation for a reading.

The section is heavily footnoted so you can read more about those concepts of special interest to you. Ideas related to handling your Tarot cards and establishing the internal and external settings are considered in Chapters 6 and 7.

Fundamental information about the various symbologies (color, numerical, astrological, and artistic) which appear on the cards is introduced in Chapter 8. Although not critical to a basic understanding of the cards—because frequently it has been included in their meanings—specific symbology can certainly amplify the messages if attended to.

Join us, now, in considering the beginning before the beginning.

Chapter 6

Tools and Talents

Loving Your Cards

Clean, attractive cards evoke positive energy and feelings of confidence and reverence, both in yourself and in anyone for whom you are reading. They convey to your own unconscious a feeling of respect for the Tarotscape which you and they will create together.

Some Tarot traditions hold that cards should be placed in a silk wrapping or bag and then stored in a wooden box. Professional readers often have two decks, one which they save for their own personal readings and one for readings for other people. Reserving a deck exclusively for your personal readings prevents other people's energies from being imprinted on your deck and allows those cards to hold your undiluted energy.

Although Steven Culbert debunks many Tarot traditions as superstitions,[29] we believe Tarot rituals serve to designate the cards or the reading as special to your inner being. This ritually established specialness increases each time you handle the cards or set up for a reading.

Actually, Culbert is concerned that heavy reliance on Tarot rituals prevents us from recognizing that it is our response to the cards' symbols which is the source of the Tarot's messages. However, the use of ritual preparation can sharpen your attunement to the cards.

So if rituals enhance your personal preparation, by all means use them. Otherwise, don't bother. Make the ritual work for you, rather than being a slave to a tradition that is meaningless to you.

Mixing It Up

The cards in a new deck are usually arranged in a sequential or hierarchical order. To prepare the cards for readings, deal them one at a time into seven separate piles and then arbitrarily restack the piles back into a complete deck. This ensures that each card will be separated from the cards that preceded and followed it in the original sequence.

---

[29] *Reveal the Secrets of the Sacred Rose,* 1988.

Mixing the cards this way also can be done between readings to ensure that the sequence of cards from a previous reading does not automatically show up in the next reading.

It's All in the Wrist

To reverse, or not to reverse; that is the question. What should we do with cards that are upside down when we turn them over? Are they somehow more, or less, important than upright cards? When you ask these questions, you step right into the middle of another long-standing Tarot debate.

Both Aleister Crowley, author of the Thoth deck, and A. E. Waite were at one time members of the esoteric Hermetic Order of the Golden Dawn, which used the Tarot in its practices. Although both men had formed their own groups by the time they created their decks, their ideas and symbolisms were rooted in the Golden Dawn tradition, which emphasized inner development and insight.

The Golden Dawn did not use reversed card meanings.[30] Although Waite did include some meanings for reversed cards in the divinatory section of his *Pictorial Key to the Tarot,* he nevertheless considered all divinatory meanings as arbitrary—the "product of secondary and uninstructed intuition"[31]—and on a lower plane from his intended use by students of the esoteric.

Today's Tarot authors differ considerably in their thoughts about how to handle, or even create, reversals in a reading. Some arrange the cards so they are all upright and caution the shuffler to take care not to reverse them. Others deliberately build a system of reversals into the deck by dividing the cards into three stacks, turning one stack upside down, combining the stacks once again, and shuffling one or more times. Still others simply shuffle the deck, taking no special pains to deliberately place cards upright or to build in reversals. Ultimately, you will have to decide for yourself which style you prefer to use.

Reversed cards are often interpreted as having "negative," or at least modified—possibly weakened—meanings, unlike upright cards. They achieve a certain significance or recognition when Tarot cards are used for divination, which Tarot for Two does not do. Rather than predicting the success or failure of your relationship efforts, Tarot for Two strives to give you insight, ways for working together, and possibilities to

[30]James Wasserman, *Instructions for Aleister Crowley's Tarot Deck,* 1978, p. 5.
[31]Arthur E. Waite, *The Pictorial Key to the Tarot,* 1986, p. 65.

consider. So for Tarot for Two readings, we place all cards upright in the layout, no matter how they turn up.

If, however, acknowledging reversed cards is important to you, then when they appear in a Tarot for Two reading, consider them as calling your attention to an idea or concept that should not be ignored.

We also like the idea of the author of *Medicine Woman Tarot,* who suggests that reversals highlight energy that is not yet fully actualized and is making its way from inner to outer expression.[32] Perhaps you have your own idea of what reversed cards signify, and find it reliable and workable for you.

Robert believes reversed cards appear when you need to pay a little extra attention to a particular heartprint position or to a card's statement, even though he ultimately places all cards upright in his Tarotscapes. Signe believes that attending to the symbology on the cards will give you far more useful inner information than attending to reversals.

When Robert does a Tarot for Two reading, he creates a conscious starting point for both himself and the querent or querents by going through both decks, one at a time, card by card, turning all the cards upright. For each deck, he then deals the cards facedown into seven piles to ensure they're thoroughly mixed. After restacking them and shuffling each deck, he passes the cards to the querents and has them shuffle their chosen decks in any way they wish. If there is only one querent, Robert represents the absent person. Querents then cut their decks, with their nondominant hands, into three stacks from right to left and restack them in any order.

Robert instructs the querents to look at the bottom card of the deck to determine which direction will be "up" for the deck. If the bottom card is upside down, he has them turn the deck so that the card's figures are upright to the persons. With this opening ritual, Robert has begun to shape the microcosm surrounding this particular reading and has started the process of directing the focus of both him and his clients toward the reading.

Signe begins her microcosmic ritual by shuffling the cards first. She then has her querents mix or shuffle them, placing them facedown when "ready." After the querent cuts the cards with his/her left hand into three piles, Signe restacks the piles into one deck, intuitively deciding the order. As she or the querents turn over each card, they place it upright in the layout.

It is traditional in Tarot readings to cut the deck into three stacks,

---

[32]Carol Bridges, *Medicine Woman Tarot,* 1989.

but readers differ as to how those stacks should be positioned. Frequently the stacks are laid out right to left. They can then be restacked from left to right, or in an intuitive order.

Sometimes the shuffling-cutting-restacking ritual is done only once. Sometimes it is repeated several times, often three. Whatever style you adopt for yourself, it is also traditional to focus on the question as you shuffle and cut the cards.

If you have decided that noting reversals is important to you, then be aware that the way you turn over the cards also affects whether your cards are upright or reversed. Whether you keep the bottom edges of the cards toward you as you turn them over, or whether you reverse the bottom edge to become the top (see Figure 2), stick with the same method throughout a given reading. Try both ways to see which seems more natural for you.

After cards have been used for a while and their surfaces have become worn, they sometimes tend to stick together when shuffled or handled. Rubbing fanning powder, available from a magician's supply shop or a magic shop, on their surfaces produces a slick, invisible finish that lets the cards slide off one another smoothly.

Different Decks

Eventually you may want to use other decks which personally appeal to you more than the Rider-Waite deck. Your readings will evoke richer responses when you read with decks that aesthetically and emotionally stimulate your unconscious symbology.

Many decks emphasize a particular type of symbology. Like his paintings, Salvador Dali's deck is rich with complex, artistic symbolism.[33] Craig Junjulas likes the Aquarian deck because its blend of ancient and modern symbols speaks to the "spirits heralding the Aquarian Age."[34]

If mythological elements speak to you and evoke your understandings of the human situation, then you may wish to work with the Mythic,[35] Arthurian,[36] or Norse[37] Tarot deck.

Many have modified the interpretations of existing decks or developed new decks which emphasize feminine or masculine orientations.

---

[33]Rachel Pollack, *Salvador Dali's Tarot*, 1985.

[34]*Psychic Tarot*, 1985, p. 7.

[35]Juliet Sharman-Burke, *The Mythic Tarot Workbook*, 1988.

[36]Caitlin and John Matthews, *The Arthurian Tarot*, 1990.

[37]Clive Barrett, *The Norse Tarot*, 1989.

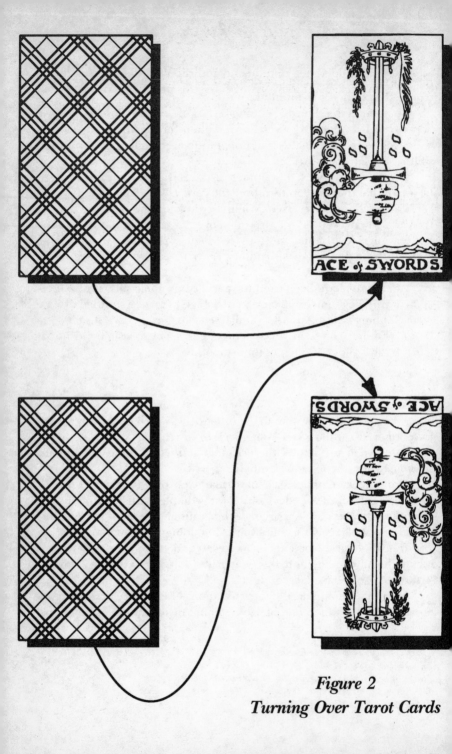

Figure 2
Turning Over Tarot Cards

Angeles Arrien added her cultural and anthropological understandings to the Thoth deck.[38] Kenneth Newman regards the Major Arcana of the Marseilles Tarot as a myth of male initiation.[39] Nik Douglas developed the Dakini deck, based on Yoga and Tantra concepts of feminine wisdom-energy.[40]

Combining decks such as the Motherpeace[41] and the Voyager[42] gives an entirely different flavor to a Tarot for Two reading. Even neo-Tarot decks, such as the "Du Wacky Du" (Morgan's Tarot),[43] can be used, but you need to consider the impact of their lightness or frivolity on the reading.

If you are interested in creating your own deck, Nancy Garen's workbook[44] emphasizes making a personal deck as a way of clarifying inner perceptions and enhancing self-confidence.

---

[38] *The Tarot Handbook*, 1987.

[39] *The Tarot. A Myth of Male Initiation*, 1983.

[40] *The Secret Dakini Oracle*, 1979.

[41] Vicki Noble, *Motherpeace: A Way to the Goddess through Myth, Art and Tarot*, 1983.

[42] James Wanless, *Voyager Tarot*, 1980.

[43] Morgan Robbins, *Morgan's Tarot*, 1983.

[44] *Complete Tarot Workbook*, 1984.

Chapter 7

Aiming for Artistry

In the Wayang Kulit shadow puppet shows of Bali, the dalang, or puppet master, is an ordained priest. He spends a great deal of time and thought beforehand, preparing himself and his puppets to tell the unfolding story.

He employs special prayers and rituals that awaken the energies of the puppets, which represent human beings in their eternal struggle between good and evil. Like a Tarot for Two reading, the Wayang Kulit performance is a symbolic microcosm.

The dalang takes great care to select which of the more than 100 puppets he will use and to arrange them appropriately for the unfolding drama. So, too, does the Tarot for Two reader need to consider the preparations that set the stage for the microcosmic drama that unfolds through the cards and results in a completed Tarotscape.

Creating Your Microcosm

Arrange an area free of distractions, in an uncluttered setting with pleasant lighting and an atmosphere of quiet and calm.

You may want to clear the reading area of negative feelings or energies. There are a number of methods for doing this, most too extensive to go into in this book. Interested readers can consult books on psychic cleansing, such as those by R. A. Ferguson,[45] Murry Hope,[46] and Draja Mickaharic.[47]

Use a flat surface large enough so the cards will not be crowded or positions overlap when laid out. Some professional readers have a special silk scarf or other cover on which they lay out the cards, establishing their microcosmic boundaries. They are in charge of this space and relate to and from it during the reading.

Experiment with secondary items and accessories, such as dimmed

---

[45] *Psychic Telemetry: New Key to Health, Wealth and Perfect Living,* 1977.
[46] *Practical Techniques of Psychic Self-Defense,* 1983.
[47] *Spiritual Cleansing,* 1982.

lights, candles, incense, flowers, crystals, or quiet music, to see if any of these is a real help to you—or merely a distraction—in developing clarity and concentration.

Some Gypsy Tarot readers place a sword or a dagger at the left of the reading area to symbolize the element of air, and to the right, a cup of water or wine, representing the element of water.[48]

While we believe that when you are reading, your concentrated attention establishes a harmonious setting, several writers are very specific about how and where you should sit for harmony.

Sergius Golowin advises the reader to sit slightly elevated and facing south, which represents life, questions, and expectation. The other person faces north, the direction of the earth and reality.[49]

Eileen Connolly suggests the same seating for two because magnetic and psychic energy currents flow along north/south lines and you will be harmonious with earth currents. She instructs, however, that when using the Tarot alone, you should face east, the direction of the rising sun and the symbolic first emanation from God.[50]

Cultivating Purposeful Awareness

Inner readiness involves switching from your everyday state of mind to one of conscious awareness of doing a reading. It means cultivating that state of alert calm within a relaxed body which fosters the intuitive process.

Experienced Tarot readers often require no more effort to do this than an experienced race-car driver notices how he changes gears. They have practiced until it becomes automatic. Like the professional racer, they shift their mental gears so effortlessly that their preparation is condensed into a single gentle breath or the momentary folding of hands.

Until you can do that, however, you might want to use meditation or relaxation techniques to clear your mind. One of the simplest techniques for inducing relaxation and inner calm is diaphragmatic breathing.

Most of us have developed an automatic pattern of breathing that has our shoulders and upper chest moving as we inhale. Shoulder breathing—sometimes referred to as "stress breathing"—expends energy unnecessarily. It is wasted effort. Thoracic (upper chest) breathing

---

[48]Sergius Golowin, *The World of the Tarot*, 1988.
[49]*The World of the Tarot*, 1988.
[50]*Tarot. A New Handbook for the Journeyman*, 1979.

not only inhibits free movement of the diaphragm, but, in fact, builds tension with each breath.

The diaphragm, attached to the bottom center of the breastbone, is actually the primary muscle involved in breathing. In diaphragmatic breathing, our chest automatically expands without effort as our lungs fill with air. Because it is one of the most efficient ways to take in maximum air with minimal effort, actors, singers, yoga students, and asthmatic patients are all taught diaphragmatic breathing.

To determine whether you are breathing stressfully or in a relaxed manner, stand in front of a mirror and observe whether your shoulders rise and fall as you inhale and exhale.

If they do, you may want to use the exercise below to help relaxed breathing become "stage one" in your inner preparation.

> ***Exercise 6—Breathing for Relaxation:*** *Sit or recline in a comfortable position with legs uncrossed. Place one hand on the chest and the other hand on the diaphragm area just below the inverted "V" of your lowest rib.*
>
> *Imagine that area as an empty balloon. Breathe so that when you inhale, the diaphragm expands and you fill that balloon. The hand covering the diaphragm moves out (or up, if reclining), while the hand on the chest remains almost still.*

Since you are not experiencing your habitual body cues, you may feel like you are not getting enough air when you practice this exercise. If so, take a couple of your usual breaths and then return to your practice. Continue practicing regularly until you can switch into diaphragmatic breathing effortlessly.

A clear and focused mind ready to interpret the language of the cards is a gift the Tarot reader brings to any reading, including her own. Use Exercise 7—or a similar one of your own—for developing focused awareness and purposeful intent prior to a Tarot reading:

> ***Exercise 7—Cultivating Purposeful Awareness:*** *Take three diaphragmatic breaths, feeling your body settle and relax.*
>
> *Repeat the following statement, or one of your own that has a similar significance:*
>
> I have only one concern during the time of this reading. I will strive to allow information to come into my consciousness and translate it into a clear, compassionate message about the

question. I offer this reading for the greatest good of everyone involved.

Repeat the three diaphragmatic breaths.

At first allow plenty of time for your mental preparation. The more frequently you practice, the easier it becomes later to automatically shift into readiness.

If the preceding exercises don't appeal to you, we nevertheless encourage you to develop a preparatory ritual, however simple or complex. Change and expand your ritual until it works for you, so that without having to deliberately think about it, you convey to your unconscious that you are moving into the intuitive, sensitive state needed to accomplish a Tarot reading.

Chapter 8
Heart Codes

Through the fusion of colors, shapes, lines, and symbols, the artist often expresses mythological themes, personal or socially prevalent philosophies, and religious or spiritual doctrines. Indeed, a prevalent belief in the Netherlands in the late-nineteenth and early-twentieth centuries was that the artist was the true visionary and prophet and that art should replace religion.

All Tarot art, no matter the deck, yields fresh riches when we delve into the intricate symbolism of its pictures. If the language of symbology is new to you, you may find it helpful to read more about the artistic and cultural nature of symbolism.[51]

In this chapter we consider various types of symbols—hidden messages—which can enrich your understanding and appreciation of the language of the Tarot. As you become more involved with your cards, we think you will want to explore those symbologies which particularly interest you, so we have heavily footnoted our material to help you get started.

Dip into this chapter as you might an appetizer, considering it not as the entire meal, but as a sampler of delicacies that whets your taste for more.

There's More to Color Than Meets the Eye

Most decks are printed in color, and our reactions to colors and their vibrations are an important part of understanding any Tarotscape. For almost as long as people have been expressing themselves artistically, colors have been carriers of symbolic meanings, serving as one way to add dimension to the message of the art. Understanding the colors on the Tarot cards enhances their emotional tone and often amplifies their significance.

Color symbolism can be modified, or amplified, by nearness or contact with other objects on the card, by objects on the card sharing the

---

[51]See, for instance, J. E. Cirlot's *A Dictionary of Symbols*, 1971; J. C. Cooper's *An Illustrated Encyclopedia of Traditional Symbols*, 1978; or the *Dictionary of Subjects and Symbols in Art* by James Hall, 1971.

same color, or by the objects depicted. Beatrex Quntanna, for instance, says the yellow background of The Fool card represents "pure intention coming from a light source," but his yellow boots symbolize having a "foundation and footing in the light and logic."[52]

On the other hand, note the places in The Fool card which are white: the sun (the holy source), the rose (feelings), the mountain peaks (truth, mental activity, mind), the dog (animal instincts), the collar or throat (spoken words), the cuffs (hands). We thank Isabel Kliegman for pointing out that these symbols' being white suggests the integration of those aspects of ourselves, all of which are holy.[53]

Although blue garments symbolize the unconscious, blue as a stream of water may change the meaning into a "stream of conscious-ness," depending on how the stream is portrayed in relation to other objects on the card.

The same or similar colors in several related cards in your Tarot-scape offer an opportunity for connection and additional insight. A pre-ponderance of light colors in one section of the Tarotscape can suggest openness and growth or, perhaps, wide-eyed willingness for adventure. An area of dark colors often warns of caution and a need to be prepared.

The remainder of this section highlights some of the more common symbolic meanings associated with Tarot card colors. We have included a blank line after each color so you can add ideas from your own per-sonal reading and understanding.

> *Exercise 8—Tapping Into Your Color Intuition: We each have our own trained responses to color. To tap into your colorful intuition, go through each card in the deck, asking:*
> 1. What reactions do I have to the colors in the cards?
> 2. How do the colors in the card expand its meaning?
> *Consider the relationship of colors to various elements and symbols of the picture, as well as how they fit into the total picture. Record your insights in your notebook.*

For additional information about specific meanings of the colors of the Major Arcana, see Beatrex Quntanna's book[54] and *Keystone of Tarot Symbols.*[55] *Keystone* offers insights into the deck developed by Paul Foster Case, which is similar to the Rider-Waite deck.

---

[52]*Tarot: A Universal Language*, 1989, pp. 29–30.
[53]Personal communication, November 13, 1990.
[54]*Tarot: A Universal Language*, 1989.
[55]Anonymous, 1979.

Color	Symbology
Red	Action; passion; courage; strength; will; pride; sensuality; desire; fire element
Rose	Love; constant affection
Orange	Energy; solar energy; spirituality; authority; mental activity; decision making
Yellow	Intellect; willpower; spiritualized intellect; mental equilibrium; caution; air element; solar (masculine) power
Green	Growth; emotion; symmetry and balance; adaptability; potential; safety; hope
Blue	Idealism; religious feelings; memory; water; receptivity; reflection; the unconscious
Violet	Spirituality; truth; healing

Color	Symbology
Purple	Royalty; authority; esoteric knowledge
Brown	Of earthly nature; potential growth
Gray	Wisdom; integration; centered; union of spirit and matter; reconciliation of opposites
Black	Power; hidden; occult; earth element; absence of light; oppression
White	Purity; openness; light
Silver	Lunar principle of reflection
Gold	Divinity; supreme law; godly thoughts; solar principle of action

One and One Is You

Whether or not you personally analyze the numerical symbologies of your Tarotscapes, it is possible, even likely, that numerology was influential in the design of the Tarot deck.[56]

Numerologists attribute different meanings to odd and even numbers. Usually, odd numbers are considered active, positive, masculine, and concerned with outward movement of the individual. They symbolize abstract concepts and idealistic concerns or endeavors. Odd numbers are sometimes regarded as divine, or as pertaining to the spiritual plane.[57]

Even numbers, considered passive by some[58] and therefore female in the archetypal sense, have been associated with the physical plane,[59] practical concepts, and everyday concerns.

The 22 letters of the Hebrew alphabet are hieroglyphs of spiritual significance and power.[60] Their numerical equivalents, which can be substituted to create a cipher, have similar significance—even said by some[61] to represent the signature of God. Both the glyphs and their representative numbers are frequently associated with the 22 Major Arcana.

In this section we offer common associations for numbers, which can help you elaborate on card meanings. But first it might help you to understand your personal reactions or associations to numbers that have been important in your life.

> **Exercise 9—Understanding Your Personal Number Symbology:** *If the symbolic understanding of numbers is new to you, you may wish to record your own associations to numbers before you read the symbologies that follow.*
>
> *Make a list of numbers from 0 to 22. Spend a few minutes thinking about each number:*
>
> 1. your experience with it
> 2. what your cultural, religious, educational, or other life experiences have taught you about it

---

[56]Robert J. O'Neill, *Tarot Symbolism*, 1986.

[57]H. A. and F. H. Curtiss, *The Key to the Universe*, 6th rev. ed., 1983.

[58]Sandor Konraad, *Numerology. Key to the Tarot*, 1983.

[59]H. A. and F. H. Curtiss, *The Key to the Universe*, 6th rev. ed., 1983.

[60]Corinne Heline, *The Bible and the Tarot*, 1969.

[61]H. A. Curtiss and F. H. Curtiss, *The Key to the Universe*, 6th rev. ed., 1983, and *The Key of Destiny*, 4th ed., 1983.

3. whether it evokes positive or negative feelings for you

4. how it does, or does not, fit into your life, past or present.

Then jot down a couple of phrases that convey that information beside each number.

The numerological associations we have compiled represent our understanding, and that of others, of the symbology of numbers. For each number we have included both spiritual and mundane meanings in no particular sequence. Following each number is a line on which you can record any new associations you learn or your personal associations from Exercise 9.

Number	*Symbology*
Zero	Boundless; pure energy; infinity; freedom from limitation; the unknowable; ultimate reality; unformed
	_____
	_____
One	The seed; the beginning; originality; initiative; independence; decision making; individuation; creativity; oneness; unity; indivisibility; the horizon; illumination
	_____
	_____
Two	Balance of opposite forces; relationships; cooperation; duality; pairs of opposites; positive and negative; reflection; receptivity; complementarity; heaven and earth
	_____
	_____

Number	*Symbology*
Three	Completion; expression; joy of living; unfolding; growth; fruits of a partnership; triune nature of man (spirit, mind, body) and divinity; manifestation; parenthood; equilibrium
Four	Order; logic and reason; classification; limitation; solidity; constructive activity; earth; the number of the physical plane (therefore of matter); the crossing of spirit and matter, i.e., unity; the four elements (earth, water, fire, and air)
Five	Midpoint between one and 10; meditation; adaptation; choices; constructive freedom; change; deciding direction; versatility; the number of humanity
Six	Double completion; two threes; balance; responsibility; love; success; equilibrium; harmony of opposites; reconciliation; urge toward perfection; idealism

Number	Symbology
Seven	Spiritual awareness; soul development; analyzing; understanding; intuition; mystical; victory; perfection; the process of mundane creation
Eight	Power, rhythm, and balance; capability; material or mundane satisfaction; work; business; the ceaseless breath of the cosmos (containing both the outbreath and the inbreath); infinity; regeneration
Nine	Giving; a triple completion; goal attainment; three threes; selflessness; humanitarianism; cycle completion; initiation; attainment on three planes (spiritual, mental, and physical); purification of heart, mind, and body; exhaustion of worldliness
Ten	See number 1 (1 + 0 = 1). Also: completed force; perfection; understanding; dominion; fully accomplished; unity; divinity; the end of a cycle, the beginning of a new cycle; the universe

After 10, many numerology systems add the integers for all numbers of two or more digits to arrive, once again, at a one-digit number ($18 = 1 + 8 = 9$, or $23 = 2 + 3 = 5$). The exceptions are double numbers, considered to be of a higher energy or vibration and, therefore, to focus on spiritual ideas.

We draw upon the works of the Curtisses and of Jerry Terranova[62] for insight into the significance of numbers above 11. Terranova refers to the numbers from one to nine as the cycle of man's development, while 11 to 19 represent the cycle of spiritualized man. We begin to apply the principles and lessons learned from the first cycle.

---

[62] *Names and Numbers: Doorways to Self-Discovery.* Unpublished manuscript, 1985.

Number	Symbology
Eleven	Illumination; insight; two ones, hence equality; a new beginning in a higher cycle; personal evolution; the initiate; pivotal point in the mystical journey (therefore, balance)
Twelve	Fruition; the manifested universe; the zodiac
Thirteen	Celestial; spiritual gathering for purpose of change or instruction; spirit manifesting on earth; transmutation

Number	Symbology
Fourteen	Mental balance; the duality of the sacred seven
Fifteen	Higher level of creativity following a 10-cycle; halfway point of spiritual creation
Sixteen	Solar eye; eye of the world; soul light
Seventeen	Expanded consciousness; the conjunction of the square or man (4) and the triangle or spirit (3), following a 10-cycle; sanctified time
Eighteen	Second initiation; turning point in personal evolution
Nineteen	Ultimate attainment; mastery of celestial or archetypal forces; spiritual wisdom; great light; the philosopher's stone

Number	Symbology
Twenty	Two cycles of 10; realized spirituality; awakened man; free will; the intelligence of will
	_____
	_____
Twenty-one	Beginning of new cycle with spirit, masculine and feminine energies, or archetypes, united; perfected man; sacred accomplishment
	_____
	_____
Twenty-two	Master builder; sharing spiritual power with others; amplification of 2 and 11; final triumph; elevation; transmutation
	_____
	_____

For an innovative way to interpret numbers in a Tarotscape, Nancy Garen[63] uses only the numbers of the Major Arcana cards appearing in the layout. Reduce the number of each Major Arcana card to its single digit (except 11 and 22)[64] and interpret *only* those numbers according to the meaning of the positions (called heartprints in the Tarot for Two Tarotscape) they occupy in the Celtic Cross spread.

Courting by the Numbers

Assigning numbers to court cards lets us use numerological principles to expand their meanings. We number our court cards by contin-

---

[63] *Complete Tarot Workbook*, 1984.
[64] In some decks The Fool is numbered 22.

uing the numerical sequence of each suit: Page = 11; Knight = 12; Queen = 13; King = 14. But Emily Peach[65] assigns the value of 7 to Pages. Knights, Queens, and Kings = 4. Aces = 5.

Look to the Heavens

Zodiac signs and planetary influences offer ideas about personal characteristics and temperament. However, when it comes to the astrological attributes of Tarot cards, authorities vary widely. Oftentimes it is difficult to tell whether this is due to the use of different decks, to different philosophies, or to changed card order (Strength and Justice cards are often reversed in various decks). Some authors assign the zodiac sign of the Hebrew letter associated with the card to the card itself.

Table 2 presents a summary of astrological attributes for the Major Arcana complied from other Tarot authors. Because we are not professional astrologers, we suggest that if you wish to incorporate astrological elements into your Tarotscapes, you pick one system, become familiar with it, and use it exclusively.

By Their Symbols Shall Ye Know Them

Although the same object may have different meanings in different cultures, many seem to be universal across cultures—the basis for Jung's theory of the "collective unconscious." Certain elements of an artist's work, or of our own dreams—our "nightly canvas"—are often related to cultural or universal meanings, yet shaped by our unique and personal experiences.

For instance, Rachel Pollack writes that it is impossible to give Salvador Dali's butterflies a constant interpretation because their meanings change with the context of the card. Dali used butterflies not only to represent the liberated spirit, but also as an element that obscures the picture sufficiently to raise anxiety.[66]

And while crutches often represent dualism, in Dali's Tower card a crutch supports an opening in the crumbling tower, permitting us "to glimpse the light of a further mystery beyond the images we know and think we understand."[67]

Careful attention to the symbolic details of a dream—or a Tarot

---

[65] *The Tarot Workbook*, 1984.

[66] Rachel Pollack, *Salvador Dali's Tarot*, 1985.

[67] Rachel Pollack, *Salvador Dali's Tarot*, 1985, p. 7.

Table 2
Selected Astrological Correlations for Major Arcana Cards of the Rider-Waite Deck Arranged by Author

Card No.	Konraad, Thierens	Junjulas, Kelen, Peach, Wang	Connolly[1]	Culbert
0			Uranus	Pluto
1	Aries/Sun	Mercury	Mercury	Sun
2	Taurus/Moon	Moon	Virgo	Moon
3	Gemini/Jupiter	Venus	Libra	Mercury
4	Cancer/Earth, Sun	Aries/Mars[2]	Scorpio	Jupiter
5	Leo/Mercury, Mars	Taurus/Venus	Jupiter	Mars
6	Virgo/Venus	Gemini/Mercury	Venus	Venus
7	Libra/Neptune, Moon	Cancer/Moon	Sagittarius	Saturn
8	Aquarius	Leo/Sun	Neptune	
9	Sagittarius/Uranus	Virgo/Mercury	Aquarius	Saturn
10	Capricorn	Jupiter/Sagittarius	Uranus	Sun, Moon
11	Scorpio/Saturn	Libra/Venus	Capricorn	
12	Pisces	Neptune	Pisces	
13	Saturn	Scorpio/Mars	Aries	
14	Mercury	Sagittarius/Jupiter	Taurus	
15	Mars	Capricorn/Saturn	Saturn	
16	Uranus	Mars/Aries	Mars	
17	Venus	Aquarius/Saturn & Uranus	Gemini	
18	Moon	Pisces/Jupiter	Cancer	
19	Sun	Sun/Leo	Leo	
20	Jupiter	Pluto/Mars	Moon	
21	Neptune	Saturn	Sun	

[1]Connolly also includes an astrological correlation for Minor Arcana cards.
[2]With the exception of card 20, Kelen follows the list of planet correlations in this column. From card 4 on, she specifies both planet and astrological signs. For card 20, she lists only Mars.

card—can entirely change our first, or superficial, understanding.

We may never be exactly sure what an artist means symbolically unless it is specifically explained. But we can begin to recognize and understand our own reactions to symbols in others' canvases as well as in the cards that comprise our own Tarotscapes.

One way to get in touch with your personal symbology for each Tarot card, and also some of the universal symbology, is to interpret the picture as if it were one of your dreams.

> *Exercise 10—Using Dream Elements to Interpret Cards:* **Using a dream interpretation technique from Gestalt therapy,[68] look at each element on the card one at a time, particularly those smaller elements which you may have disregarded before.**
>
> *Begin your interpretation by stating, "I am . . . [some element on the card] and I am . . . [describe yourself]. My function is to . . . [describe your purpose or responsibility]."*
>
> *Continue with at least two more sentences about yourself as that element on the card. Then repeat the process for every element on the card.*
>
> *Judgment interferes with the intuitive process. So, at this point in your thinking, do not judge whether the understandings that arise relate primarily to you or whether they reflect a more universal knowledge to which all persons can relate. You can sort that out later.*

Applying the above exercise, we looked at the Two of Pentacles in the Rider-Waite deck. Focusing on the blue, wavy lines in the background, we began:

> *I am the blue, wavy lines behind the juggler. I am in his background, so I am always with him. My function is to remind him from time to time that there are ups and downs in this juggling act called life. But I am pretty even in my construction, so I remind him that even those ups and downs will not be too traumatic and will be balanced.*
>
> *I am the large ship on those waves. Two of my sails are yellow and two are red, showing that while I am sailing through life, I employ a balance of reason (yellow) and passion (red). I am heading into a low, but I can see the smaller ship ahead of me and realize that I will soon be riding the crest.*

---

[68]Fritz Perls, *Gestalt Therapy Verbatim,* 1969.

We stopped with two items for purposes of this example, but ideally, you should continue with every item on the card.

Don't be surprised if many clichés automatically occur to you during this process. It is another sign that your personal symbolic understandings are rising to the surface, for our unconscious processes often make use of clichés, rhythms, rhymes, and puns. This is called "primary process" thinking, as opposed to logical thinking, and is also the language of dreams.

After you have explored your own symbolic understanding of a card's elements, you may enjoy comparing it with the understandings of others.

For instance, looking up "waves" in *A Dictionary of Symbols,*[69] we read that in Chinese tradition the rhythmic undulations of waves symbolize dragons and the white foam suggests purity. The dragon symbolism does not immediately connect, but the term "rhythmic undulations" once again suggests the cycle of balance.

We found no entry for "waves" in *An Illustrated Encyclopedia of Traditional Symbols,*[70] but did find an extensive entry for "water" which included many cultural and religious symbologies that enhanced our understanding of balance as depicted on this card, i.e., water is equated with flux, with regeneration, and has both life-giving and life-taking aspects.

As you explore each card, take nothing for granted. Notice it; question it. Why, for instance, are the suns on The Fool, The Lovers, Death, The Sun, and The Moon[71] cards so different? Surely this is no accident. To help you in your search, become the sun in each card—as in Exercise 10 above—and speak about yourself. Get acquainted with your function.

Studying the symbology of other cultures and reading about what other authors write concerning symbology in general, as well as the symbology of Tarot cards, will also add to your understanding of hidden meanings. Many writers connect Tarot symbology with Hebrew mysticism. According to Jason Lotterhand,[72] for instance, following the outline of the arms and shoulders on The Magician card creates a Yod, the first stroke of the first letter—creation, creativity, enterprise. Other cards on which Yods appear as leaves, droplets of waters, and flames are The

---

[69]J. E. Cirlot, 2nd ed., 1971.
[70]J. C. Cooper, 1978.
[71]Some readers believe The Moon card actually shows an eclipse of the sun.
[72]*The Thursday Night Tarot,* 1989.

Moon, The Tower, Ace of Cups, Ace of Swords, and Ace of Wands.[73]

Before you read further, take a moment to look at these cards and see what sense you make of their Yods and to check Yod symbology near the end of this chapter. Now, how do you think Yods expand on the meanings of the cards?

Hint: Yods definitely show up at beginnings or times of transition. They're creative life power; building blocks that remind us of "higher" interventions, perhaps from our own deities, our inner guides, or the collective wisdom of our community or culture.

Speak as their different colors and determine how that modifies their meaning for you. Pat yourself on the back if you also noticed the differing number and placement of the Yods.[74]

A symbology we've seen very little written about with respect to Tarot cards concerns mudras—ritual hand gestures which represent a mantra or a magic formula. They initiate action or hold a focus of attention.

In both Hawaiian and Balinese dances, for instance, the movements of the dancers' hands are not incidental or merely rhythmically beautiful. They tell part of the story, and to "read" them is to add another dimension to your understanding of the performance.

In addition to the most noticeable mudra in the Ten of Swords (see our card meaning), we also have found mudras in The Hierophant and the Six of Pentacles (the same mudra, which symbolizes "all is not revealed"), The Lovers, The Devil, The Magician, the Four of Swords, and, possibly, the Seven of Cups.

Take your cards out and look at the firm way the sword is held in the Justice card and in those cards in the Swords suit where the sword is held. But notice the right-hand gesture of the foreground figure in the Five of Swords. It is the only card in which the forefinger does not grasp the sword, but, rather, forms a mudra.

Exercise 11—Mudras in the Suit of Pentacles: *Examine the variety of ways pentacles are held by the people depicted in that suit. How do their hand positions add to your understanding of what the characters are expressing?*

---

[73]Some writers describe The Hierophant's crown as composed of Yods. In Paul Foster Case's deck, the cap on The Hermit takes the Yod form.

[74]If you wish still more information on Yods in the Tarot, see Daphna Moore, *The Rabbi's Tarot*, 1987.

Authors who have written on the symbology of the Tarot cards include Betty Kelen,[75] Jason Lotterhand,[76] Beatrex Quntanna,[77] and Robert O'Neill.[78] O'Neill enriched our understanding of The Devil card by pointing out that the devil has a navel. He is born of woman, therefore, and is not meant to be regarded as a god, fallen angel, or spirit. As portrayed, he is our archetypal shadow, the dark side within each of us that must be acknowledged and faced before we can complete our inner growth.

We have compiled the symbol meanings in this section to facilitate your understanding of the Tarot cards. Our listing is by no means complete.

Remember, the symbolic meanings of elements on a card may vary depending on their location in the picture, their color, their proximity to other elements, and any action in which they may be used. Once again, we have provided lines on which to enter your own associations, which we hope will continue to expand the longer you work with the Tarot.

---

[75] *The Language of the Tarot,* 1974.
[76] *The Thursday Night Tarot,* 1989.
[77] *Tarot: A Universal Language,* 1989.
[78] *Tarot Symbolism,* 1986.

Element	Symbology
angel	messenger from creator; intermediary; pure being; invisible forces; guardian
apprentice	helper; learner; novice; trainee
arbor	cover; passageway; blessing
arch	doorway; vagina; initiation; memorial
arm	strength; invocation. Different positions symbolize: work, protection, supplication, offering, surrender.
armor	protection; defense; invincibility; chivalry; all-conquering (Steel armor is a symbol of Mars.)
army	comrades; fighters; defenders

Element	Symbology
artisan	master; craftsman
astrological signs	power; personality traits
balance	equality; justice; equilibrium; impartiality
ball	world; completion; sun; moon; wholeness
bandage	wound; covering; insignia
banner	identity; action; passionate connection to life; victory; power
baton	leadership; wand; authority
battle	winner; loser; strife; hurt

Element	Symbology
beard	wisdom; age; dignity; virility; sovereignty; masculinity; completed experience
bed	comfort; safety; rest (see also "sleep")
bedspread	map of consciousness; cover; warmth; security
bee	fruitfulness; honey; diligence; social organization; cleanliness; immortality; soul; purity (Many additional meanings, depend on cultural or religious beliefs.)
belt	protection; binding power; strength
birds	spirits; souls; ideas; freedom; mediators between heaven and earth
blindfolded	lack of insight and understanding; ignorance; absence of knowledge

Element	Symbology
blood	life; passion; life principle; soul; strength; sacrifice
books	knowledge; learning; study; wisdom; law; book of life; a quest; what is hidden and what is revealed
boots	protection; strength; liberty
bound; binding	restrained; caught; held back
boy	initiate; inexperienced
breasts	motherhood; nourishment; protection; abundance of love; fertility
breasts, bared	truth; free and natural; freedom

Element	Symbology
bridge	access; path; link between one realm and another; the passage to reality; initiation; transition; separation between opposites; change
bridle	restrain; control
bull	steadfast; power; strength; ambivalent; male procreative strength; royalty; the earth; the moon
butterfly	soul; immortality; freedom; metamorphosis; rebirth
buttons	sun; moon; closure; status; ornamentation
camp	home; mobile home; nature
cap	cover; freedom; power; nobility; thoughts

Element	Symbology
castle	fortress; home; power; spiritual testing; watchful spiritual power; defended city
cat	helper; companion; independent; moon; stealth; luck (good or bad, depending on color and cultural values); mysterious splendor; repose
chains	restraint; prisoner; bonds; communication; marriage; social or psychic integration; destiny; cause and effect
cherub; cherubim	angel child; innocence; presence of divinity; guardian of the sacred
child	inner child; playmate; playfulness; innocence; purity; potentials; simplicity; dependent; available energy; curious; undeveloped; impulsive
child, nude	truth; nothing to hide; openness; vulnerability

Element	Symbology
circle	life; the world; completion; sun; eternity; heaven; perfection; totality; integration; self-contained; the divinity (Takes on additional meanings, depending on color, and on elements attached to or within it.)
city	communal life; sophistication; shelter; feminine principle; embodiment of sacred geometry
cloak	dignity; rank; disguise; hiding true nature; protection; the acquired self (outer image)
clouds	water; storm; thoughts; illusion; veiling; prophecy; messenger
clown	exaggeration; the fool; frivolity; laughter; fun; caricature
coat	cover; warmth; security; achievement and status

Element	Symbology
coffin	mystic womb; spirit buried in matter; the physical plane; redemption; salvation; death; an ending; transformation; regeneration; rebirth
coin	trade; power; status; ability to pay; attitudes toward money
crayfish	armored consciousness; primordial; evolution; instinctive energy
crosier	staff of power; guidance; jurisdiction; mercy; faith
crown	sovereignty; victory; honor; authority; integration; endless continuity; energy and power of the head; success; spiritual attainment; worldly power; identification; false authority
crutch	support; help; lameness; moral shortcoming

Element	Symbology
cube	stability; the material world; earth; final state of a cycle; immobility; truth; static perfection; crystallization; the element of salt
cup	receptive; passive; feminine form; the draught of life; plans; sensuality; feelings; love; nourishment; overflowing abundance
cup, overturned	emptiness; vanity; loss; plans gone awry
curtain	cover; hidden; separation; pre-enlightened state; illusion of manifest world; esoteric or mysterious knowledge; concealment; protection
cushions	acknowledgment and acceptance of passionate nature; support; ease (Meaning changes, depending on placement and pattern shown.)
dance	transformation of time and space; movement; rhythm of universe; change; grace; becoming; act of creation

Element	Symbology
darkness	primordial chaos; unmanifested light; state of transition; germination; mystical nothingness (no-thing); mystery; things hidden; fear
dawn	illumination; hope; resurrection; rebirth; enlightenment
death	transformation; change; end of an epoch
disk	sun; renewal of life; perfection; divinity; power; immortality; cycles
dog	fidelity; watchfulness; guardian; keeper of boundaries; intermediary between moon deities; guide; evolving nature; trained intellect
door	hope; opportunity; passage from one state or world to another; initiation; access to feminine mysteries
dove	life spirit; soul; peace; innocence; gentleness; chastity; reconciliation

Element	Symbology
eagle	sun; power; flight; clear sight; ascension; inspiration; father; release from bondage; the element of air; the emotional plane
earth	Great Mother; resources; nourisher; inexhaustible creativity; sustenance; nurturing; natural; ground rules made apparent
eclipse	to overshadow; cover; usurp; come before; to obscure; pass in front of briefly
egg	life principle; germ of creation; undifferentiated totality; mystery of life; universal; birth; the universe; potentiality; latent; womb
ellipse	the cosmic egg; womb; involution and evolution; path of return; gateway
Eucharist	consecrated; blessing; sharing; union; sacrifice; wisdom; spiritual or vital power; memorial

Element	Symbology
evergreen	immortality; vitality; the eternal; generative power
eye	omniscience; inner sight; all-seeing; intuitive vision; light; enlightenment; knowledge; vision; perception; the seer and the seen
family	connected; security; home; bliss; acceptance; culture and traditions
feet/foot	freedom of movement; willing service; humility; treading down of worldly passions and existence; understanding; roots
field	the earth mother; the great provider; nourisher; limitless potentiality; openness and perspective
fingers	power; spiritual power (when fingers raised in benediction); will (index finger); duality (when second and third fingers parted); numbers; counting

Element	Symbology
fire/flame	transformation; life; purification; destruction; gift; heat; passion; spiritual energy
fish	emerging consciousness; procreation; the watery element; psychic being; life force; profound life; fecundity; devotees and disciples; spiritual nourishment
flight/flying	transcendence; passing from the conditioned to the unconditioned; spiritual release; freedom; movement; thought; imagination
flowers	the feminine; passive principle; fruition; transitoriness; happy growth; the soul; blossoming of potential (Meaning modified, depending on color and shape of flower.)
forest	nature; growth; hidden; realm of the psyche; feminine principle; a place of testing and initiation; the secrets of nature; the unconscious
fountain	mother source; instruction; refreshment; life force; mystic center; individuality; soul as the source of spiritual energy; joyful

Element	Symbology
friends	companions; support
garden	paradise; organized nature; soul; food supply; abundance; home of creatures; consciousness; life
garland	joy; happiness; dedication; badge; good luck; linking everything in universe; fruitfulness
grapes	wisdom; food; wine; drink; nourishment; fruits of labor; fertility; sacrifice
hair	life force; strength; energy; power of thought; virility; energy; lower or base powers (body hair); higher forces (head hair); freedom (hair flowing loose)
halo	enlightenment; awareness; vital energy of wisdom; virtue; saintliness
hand	tool of tools; expression; communication; help; trust; manifestation; action (Meaning changes, depending on position.)

Element	Symbology
hat	authority; power; status; thought; differentiation of social status; covering; protection
hawk	predator; power; transformation; the soul
heart	love; life; center of being; vitality; eternity; wisdom of feeling
helmet	protection; preservation; hidden thoughts (if visor lowered); lofty thoughts (if visor open)
hood	concentration of spiritual power; self-concealment; initiatory rites
horns	supernatural power; divinity; animal nature; beast; strength and power
horse	intense desires and instincts; intellect; wisdom; reason; burden carrier; nobility; dynamic power; fleetness; the cosmos; intuitive understanding

Element	Symbology
horse, charging	attack; movement; unleashed energy
ibis	the soul; aspiration; perseverance; transformation of consciousness; wisdom; truth; justice
ice	frozen consciousness; rigidity; frigidity; impermanence; brittleness; dividing boundary (as between the conscious and the unconscious); clarity; changeability
iris	power of light; hope; truth; promise; message from another realm; illumination; royalty
keys	powers of opening and closing; mystery; liberation; knowledge; initiation; clues; solution to problem
lamp/lantern	life; light; wisdom; intelligence; inner spirit; guidance; good works; presence of divinity; illuminating

Element	Symbology
laurel	triumph; inner or outer victory; chastity; truce; fecundity
lightning	spiritual illumination; enlightenment; revelation; the descent of power; sudden realization of truth; destruction of ignorance; critical condition; unleashed energy; instability; dynamic power
lily	purity; peace; resurrection; royalty; enlightenment; truth
lily pads	steps; home; humility; islands of security
lingam	phallus; creativity; masculine generative principle
lion	solar; majesty; strength; courage; fortitude; justice; law; military might; virility; masculine principle

Element	Symbology
lizard	lunar creature; silence; divine wisdom; completed cycle (when shown biting tail); soul; renewal
	_____
	_____
magic wand	power; creativity; authority; potential; directing energies
	_____
	_____
merchant	owner; seller; buyer; transmitter of customs
	_____
	_____
monks	disciples; probationers; student and/or master
	_____
	_____
moon	female; cycles; unconscious; fertility; horns of power (when shown as crescent); magnetic forces; receptivity; intuition; imagination
	_____
	_____
mountain	height of awareness; isolation; loneliness; peak experiences; spiritual retreat; expanding universe; challenge
	_____
	_____
night	ending; ignorance; loss; lost; dread; silent; passive principle; the unconscious; potential; germination; anticipation; sleep
	_____
	_____

Element	Symbology
nimbus	See "halo."
nude figures	natural; innocent; openness; truth; pure; nothing to hide
olive branch	peace; fruitfulness; plenty; reconciliation
path	the way; path of life; direction; travel; following the lead of others
pentacle	sign of man; magic; earth; wealth; form
pentagram (five-pointed star)	(When upright): life; aspiration; light; the spiritual; guide; education. (When reversed): evil; witchcraft; black magic; sign of the devil
pillars	support; guards; world axis; standing firm; spinal column

Element	Symbology
pitcher, pouring	abundance; choice; cosmic waters; feminine nourishing principle; acceptance; fertility; the heart
planets	the various forces of the universe and nature; cycles; homes
plants	the cycle of life; food; cycles; fertility; mystery of death and resurrection
plowed earth	cultivated; ready to grow; receptive
pomegranate	fruitfulness; fertility; the oneness of the universe
puddles	held and restricted thoughts; need for caution
pumpkin	harvest; empty-headed; link between upper and lower worlds

Element	Symbology
pyramid	earth; center axis; sacred mountain; power; energy; creation
rabbit	lunar animal; speed; sexuality; trickster
rain	cleansing; fertilization; life; purification; heaven-sent; spiritual influences; renewal; fresh beginning; expression of feelings
rainbow	heavenly glory; different states of consciousness; meeting of heaven and earth; bridge; forgiveness; happiness; gift
ram	virility; masculine; power; sacred; sacrifice
river	flow; movement; unconscious; return to the source; fertility; irreversible passage of time; transitory
robe	protection; achievement; status

Element	Symbology
rock	permanence; stability; reliability; obstacles; coldness; hardness; the eternal; the cosmos; marker of sacred places or events; altar; foundation
rose	(Meaning modified as color of blossom and number of petals change): heavenly perfection; earthly passion; love; fertility; completion; the mystic center; voluptuousness; sensuality; idealized; unfolding; seduction
sails	the spirit as breath or wind; fortune; increasing power; the element of air
sand	instability; impermanence; infinity; unnumbered; shifting
scales of justice	balance; equality; justice; harmony; measurement
scepter	divine or royal power; sovereignty; phallic; transmission of life force; fertility; supreme authority

Element	Symbology
scroll	learning; knowledge; law; book of life; passage of time
scythe	death; time; harvest; ambiguity (of the beginning as the end)
sea	feminine; unconscious; acceptance; inner knowing; vital energy; dissolving; infinity; travel
seeds	life; abundant possibilities; alternating cycles; rebirth; potential growth; beginnings; latent forces; mysterious potentialities
serpent	energy; force; cycles of manifestation; passion; wisdom; healing; poison; resurrection; sexual energy; instinct; fear
shells	feminine principle; birth; regeneration; life; love; marriage; fertility; safe travel; good luck
shield	preservation; protecting feminine power; emblem

Element	Symbology
ship	transcending the material plane; the feminine vessel of transformation; adventure; transportation; ship of life; travel
	_____
	_____
shovel	path clearer; tool; mover; digger
	_____
	_____
silhouette	in shadow; hidden; in darkness; contrast; separation
	_____
	_____
skull	transience; the transformational process; protective; seat of thought and spirit; fear associated with change
	_____
	_____
sky	transcendence; infinity; height; the heavens; cover; spirit; mental realm; cosmic rhythms
	_____
	_____
sleep	unconscious; rest; dreams
	_____
	_____
snail	resurrection; renewal; cyclic development
	_____
	_____

Element	Symbology
sphere	perfection; total of all possibilities; cosmic egg; cycles; ether or heaven
	_____
	_____
sphinx	enigma; power; vigilance; strength; combination of physical and intellectual powers; the four elements; synthesis of all past sciences
	_____
	_____
square	the earth; plane of existence; static perfection; honesty; integrity; morality; straightforwardness
	_____
	_____
stars (for single star, see pentagram)	divinity; supremacy; the eternal; messenger of God; hope; aspiration; light; creation; the spiritual; guide; inspiration; seeking; discovery
	_____
	_____
stream	consciousness; life-giving power; movement
	_____
	_____
sun	supreme cosmic power; all-seeing; center of being; intuitive knowledge; life; light; heroic principle at its brightest; optimism; radiating; vitalizing; energetic
	_____
	_____

Element	Symbology
sunflower	new growth; worship; soul; sun; majesty; enlightenment
sunrise/ sunset	the beginning and the ending; cycles; spiritual journey
tents	temporary home; nomadic dwelling; enveloping (especially secrets or divine knowledge)
throne	seat of authority; stability; world center; unity; synthesis
tower	bastion of truth; end of a cycle; gaining perspective; focused attention; meditation; transcendence; ascent; shelter; protective; the human body; structure of the unconscious
tree	the whole of manifestation; synthesis of heaven, earth, and water; dynamic life; growth; developed knowledge; stability; shelter; the union of earth and heaven; the nervous system

Element	Symbology
triangle	the Trinity; the threefold nature of the universe; upward aspiration (when pointing upward); life; fire; flame; heat
valley	neutral zone; fertile; creation; life; progress; mystical home of priests; rest; descent
veil	darkness; predawn; pre-enlightened; hidden or esoteric knowledge; secrecy; concealment; ignorance
vine/ vineyard	abundance; life; passion; fertility; clinging; creeping; branching
wall	threshold; enclosure; protection; stability; barrier
water	source of all; consciousness (surface of water); unconscious (watery depths); dissolution; purity; cleanliness; potentialities; ablution; fertility; universal solvent; overwhelming; fluid (potential for change); movement

Element	Symbology
waves	ceaseless motion; purity (white foam); change; illusion; vanity; agitation; movement; disturbance; rhythm
wheat	food; abundance; harvest; fertility
wheel	solar power; cycles; inner movement; mobility; change; experience
window	open to outside influences; a way to see; consciousness; receptivity; possibilities; limitation; personal viewpoint
window, stained glass	enlightened viewpoint; spirituality; aspiration; heavenly abundance
wings	flight; ability to overcome; spirituality; imagination; freedom; victory; swiftness; intelligence; swift messenger; spiritual evolution
wolf	the earth; untamed; uncivilized; evil; scavenger

Element	Symbology
wreath	victory; glory; supremacy; dedication; wholeness; completion; happy fate; merit; success
world	earth; everything; position; status; existence
Yod	the origin; gift; flame; beginning; spirit into matter
yoke	union; control; balance; discipline; obedience; sacrifice
zodiac	relationship in the universe; wheel of life; 12 personality types

Part 4

Tarot For Two

Tarot Tutor 4

Tarot for Two in action. The turn of their wrists 11 times and two people have a fresh perspective on their relationship. More than that, they have been called upon to interact differently during the debut of their Tarotscape.

As Peter Balin said in his introductory essay, growth initiates crisis. A truly memorable creation—be it a dance, a play, a film, or a painting—disturbs us, calls upon us to ponder its implications. Just as our tongue can never ignore the hole left by that newly lost tooth, our Tarotscapes nudge us to probe their themes and ideas for relevancy.

So far we've been extolling the virtues of the Tarot for Two; now it's your turn to see for yourself. Part 4 teaches you the specifics of doing Tarot for Two readings and creating Tarotscapes for examining your relationships.

Chapter 9 details how the Tarotscape cross and staff forge the framework of your relationship and also presents guidelines for when to work with someone and when to work alone.

Suggestions for formulating your question and deciding which decks to use are considered in Chapter 10. Card meanings are modified by the heartprint—Chapter 11—each card occupies in the Tarotscape. Chapter 12 presents a step-by-step procedure for creating and interpreting your Tarotscapes.

Using worksheets is one of the quickest ways to sharpen and expand your Tarotscape outlook. We employ the worksheet formats introduced in Chapter 13 for presenting the example Tarotscapes of Part 5. In addition, Appendix 4 contains one of our student's interpretations of a Tarot for Two reading using the worksheets.

And you—what are *your* dreams? What fantasies and concerns will rise from your inner longings and express themselves in your Tarotscapes? It's time to find out.

Pathways for Partnering

Relationships, the way we feel about them and the way we react within them—or run from them—are the heart of everything we do: parent-child relationships, sibling relationships, teacher-student relationships, love relationships, work relationships, friendships, and even the relationships we have with projects and deities.

Through relationships we receive the love and support we need to thrive, the gratifications we need to feel successful. It is also through relationships that we experience the inevitable stresses and frustrations that help us strive and grow, or overwhelm us to the point of ending the relationship.

Certainly all relationships have at least two sides to the story. Each of us brings into our relationships the victories and scars of past relationships—our trophies and our excess baggage. Your Tarotscape pinpoints their interplay in your particular relationship.

Using a different size or shape of Tarot cards for each person offers you visual insight into the dynamics of your interaction. Having both cards—both attitudes—simultaneously visible in each heartprint gives equal representation to the feelings and emotional involvement of each person.

As the reading unfolds, the Tarot for Two often identifies differing motivations behind the issue and clarifies satisfactions and frustrations. While the Tarot for Two works for all questions involving social, romantic, business, or family relationships, it is a natural for mates or lovers.

Figure 3 shows the layout and card placement of the Tarot for Two spread. The cards are numbered according to the sequence in which they are drawn and placed in the Tarotscape.

Through a Tarot for Two reading, and the resulting Tarotscape, you explore your relationship questions by considering the meaning of each card relative to its specific heartprint. Each card/heartprint interface in the Tarotscape provides a specific insight about your question or issue.

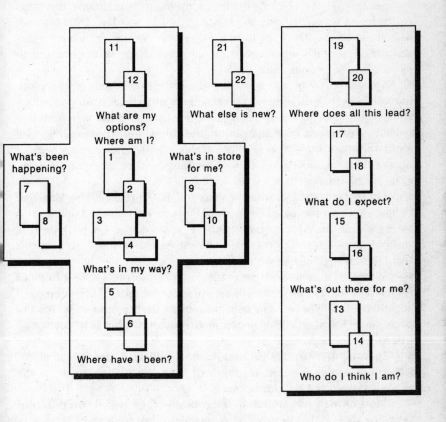

Figure 3
Layout and Card Placement of Tarot for Two

Many Tarot readers use a significator card, which establishes and represents the querent in the reading. There are probably as many ways to select a significator as there are Tarot readers.

Sometimes the reader will choose the card from among the court cards, based on comparing the age, sex, and hair color of the querent with those of the figure on the card. Some select the suit which represents the querent's astrological sun sign and then ask the querent to choose one of its four court cards.

Querents may be asked to select the court card which "feels" more like them at that time or which represents a particular attitude or approach to life or to the issue in question. Queens symbolize feminine principles of dominance and power; and Kings, similar masculine principles. Knights may represent principles of assertiveness, aggression, service/help, or movement. Pages often represent children or the inner child of the querent.

On the other hand, some readers will always choose The Magician or The Emperor for male clients and The High Priestess or The Empress as the significator for women. Others may ask the querent to look through the deck and purposefully choose a card, or simply draw a card from the fanned, face-down deck.

Whatever the method, the reader usually interprets the meaning of the card as representing the power, mood, or attitude of the querent. It sets the tone of the reading and influences the manner in which the question is answered. The selection process may also help focus and orient the querent.

In using the Tarot for divination, the significator card says, in effect, "If you are this [the significator card], then here [the layout] is the predicted outcome to your question."

Most of the groupings and descriptions of the people on the court cards by hair and skin color were made in the context of European backgrounds. When selected as reflections of outer appearances rather than inner states, they frequently are not appropriate in today's multi-ethnic society. Further, for Tarot for Two purposes, selecting a significator—be it a court card, Major Arcana card, or any other in the deck—removes that card from a possible role in the spread.

In a Tarot for Two reading, therefore, the work of the significator card—and the selection ritual—is replaced by the choice of decks and by the careful creation of the question. Your question helps you formulate where you are in your expression of personal power and gives you an opportunity to refine your role and strength.

When you first start out with a general question, as most of us do, you usually are not as focused as you might be. The more you shape and refine your question until you have it exactly the way you want it, the more you gather the power to create the answer to your now-specific question. (See Chapter 10 for more help in formulating your question.)

What is significant in a Tarot for Two reading is your ability to consider alternatives and then adapt or modify your approach according to information gleaned from the entire layout.

My Cross and My Staff, They Enlighten Me

The Tarotscape cross clarifies the attitudes and experiences each of you brings to the situation. It shows your individual and unique pathways and how your experiences enhance or interfere with the present situation. Comparing your separate experiences aids you in identifying conflicts and cooperation styles.

The staff symbolizes support, energies you have available to draw on. The eight staff cards in the Tarot for Two layout (four cards from each deck) show your respective abilities to implement the insights of the Tarotscape.

They pinpoint inner perceptions which you may not have recognized or outwardly revealed. They offer you the opportunity to identify discrepancies and to examine how your sense of self cooperates with or sabotages the question you want resolved.

Your individual staffs reflect the support each of you has available for the other. Neither of you has to resolve the question alone. You can work together, drawing upon your staff resources.

Comparing staff cards with cross cards helps identify the difference between your personal sense of self (staff cards) and your outward behavior (cross cards).

Someone to Watch Over Me

Whatever the nature of our relationships, we enter into them with expectations, some of which are known to us and some of which are hidden. Since they are the source of much satisfaction as well as the basis for many frustrations, the What do I expect? heartprint deals specifically with expectations.

Love relationships in particular foster expectations of commitment and loyalty and harbor disappointments as our partners fail, in numerous little ways, to meet our expectations.

Marriage counselors say that love is frequently the least of our reasons for selecting a mate. We may select a love partner because we need to be nurtured in a particular way. Oftentimes we imagine the other can satisfy unmet childhood needs, complement lost or undeveloped parts of ourselves, be eternally available, or make us whole.

The more expectations we identify for ourselves and make known to the other(s)—not only in the love relationship, but in all relationships—the better basis we have for understanding and fulfillment. Making expectations explicit is a critical step in resolving conflict through negotiation and compromise rather than via manipulation.

P.S. I Love You

At our option, we often use an additional two cards to summarize the reading or to present supplemental information. They are like a postscript, a P.S., to the Tarot for Two spread. They ask the heartprint question "What else is new?"

Just as we often add a last, important thought to our letters—an essential point that has just occurred to us after we've finished the other business in the letter—so, too, the last two cards in your Tarotscape direct you to an issue you might have otherwise missed, or might not have been ready, until now, to consider.

Don't Spread It Around

If you are reading for anyone else but yourself, we think the reading should be confidential, so don't go blabbing what you've learned to others. Naturally, you are free to share information from readings about your own relationships, unless your partner asks otherwise.

When you read for friends, tell them the reading offers suggestions, options, and possibilities, not guarantees or predictions. The purpose of the reading is to clarify feelings and motivations which can affect the question and which offer possibilities for growth.

Know Thy Limitations

Although the Tarot for Two is designed to reveal feelings and attitudes of two persons, a reading with both parties present may not always be the most productive approach and should not be entered into casually.

Advantages to working through the spread together include:

- Gaining a common insight into the question.
- Revelations concerning attitudes you and your partner may hold.
- Enhanced communication as you approach your joint issue from a different perspective.

Two people should not do a Tarot for Two together when:

- One of them is so concerned with appearing "good" or "right" that his/her attitudes may distort the session.
- One of you feels inhibited in the presence of the other and, therefore, unable to be candid. This in itself may pinpoint your problem.

Chapter 10

Bridging the Threshold

Most, if not all, religions share a belief in the dualism between the realms of heaven and earth. Mythologies distinguish between "sacred space" for the gods, or the holy, and "profane space," where the rest of us live. A threshold, often with a guardian, separates the two.

In Icelandic mythology, for example, a rainbow bridge made of fire, air, and water arches from earth, Midgard, to Asgard, where the gods reside. It is guarded by Heimdall, who never needs sleep and has incredible vision and hearing.

Another threshold appears in one of the most famous dreams from the Bible. Jacob sees angels ascending and descending a ladder reaching into heaven.

Threshold symbology also serves to express the distinction between the unknown and human awareness, which in psychological terms are called the unconscious and the conscious. All Tarotscapes bring myth into reality by bridging the threshold between the two realms. The very act of creating a Tarotscape opens your awareness and awakens you to new understandings.

One of the major goals of a Tarot for Two reading is to help you see the situation in another light. When you have accomplished that, you have bridged the threshold.

Ask and You Shall Receive

Whether your issue involves romance, family, work, home, or any other relationship, all Tarotscapes begin with the formulation of a specific question. By establishing our focus for exploration, the question steers us between what we know in our conscious awareness and the reservoirs of information in our unconscious.

Much as the knights of old needed to properly formulate a question before they could successfully embark on their quest, you, too, need to carefully formulate your question. Asking the right question sets up a conscious resonance which, like the magical fairy-tale phrase "open sesame," facilitates access to your unconscious treasures and aids you in arriving at the right conclusion.[79]

The more precise you make your question, the more effectively you bridge the threshold. When you formulate the question that resonates with your heart's wish to know, you set up a sympathetic vibration to the appropriate answer. They come together in the pictures and meanings of the cards you draw.

In several places in this book we make the analogy between interpreting the Tarot for Two and putting together a picture puzzle. Your question is the border of the puzzle. It allows you to begin filling in the center of the puzzle, the core of your issue. Without it, completing the picture takes a lot longer.

A thoughtfully constructed question plus information from the cards transforms your question into a working hypothesis. If two of you work together, keep revising the question until you both agree it expresses exactly what you want to know. Once the question is formed, state it out loud one last time before beginning to create your Tarotscape.

Since the Tarot for Two is not used for divination, but rather to assist you in delving into your own inner wisdom, questions should not be ones which can be answered with a "yes" or a "no." For instance, the question "Will I meet my true love at tonight's party?" can be answered "Yes" or "No" and does not need the intricacy of a Tarot for Two reading. But questions like "If I meet my true love tonight, what will our relationship be like?" or "If I meet my true love tonight, what issues do I need to be aware of?" are appropriate ones for a Tarot for Two reading.

A common kind of question that querents bring to professional readers is something like "Is Tom really serious about me?" or "I just met a very nice man who seems interested in me. Is this going to develop into anything?"

Although these questions are phrased for a "yes" or a "no" answer, you can restructure your question to probe the issue in a more comprehensive way. Use questions like:

What are the things about our relationship that are most important to Tom?

What is holding us back from getting serious?

How can I encourage this acquaintance into a deeper friendship?

What kind of approaches can I make that won't scare him off?

---

[79]Georgia Lambert R. Personal communication, April 16, 1990.

While most of us would desperately like a simple answer to the question of whether or not we are falling in love with someone—especially when we are in the throes of new or conflicting feelings and indecision—to ask "Am I falling in love with Allen?" is, once again, not the most effective way to use the Tarot for Two. Rather, better questions would be:

What's happening between Allen and me?
What are the issues Allen and I need to consider to develop a better relationship?
Where is our relationship headed?
What do I need to consider to be more desirable to Allen?
What do I need to be aware of that Allen considers important?

Likewise, questions such as "Will I find love on my vacation?" or "Will I go on vacation this year?" need to be reoriented to questions like:

What will I discover on my vacation?
What will I face on my vacation?
What do I need to consider to get the most out of my vacation?

With these questions, you're really asking about your relationship with a project, your vacation. Questions related to people might be phrased as:

What issues will I have to face (or, more simply, what will happen) if I take a vacation with Molly (or Jill or Richard, etc.)?
If I meet an interesting woman (or man) on my vacation, what should I keep in mind?

Being complex human beings, we always bring all of our past experiences, our current situation, and our hopes for the future into any relationship. To clarify how our "all-too-human situation" affects a relationship, we could ask questions such as:

What am I bringing into this relationship that may hinder it?
What am I bringing into this relationship that may strengthen it?
What influences are affecting my fears (or hopes, or dreams) about this relationship?
What motivating factors do I need to be more aware of to better understand the relationship?

Your focus in formulating Tarot for Two questions needs to be one of asking what you need or want to know about a particular person or relationship. Your questions would direct you to explore relationship issues while you review the candidates, say, for your love. Your cards answer by telling you what you need to know about another, what he or she needs to know about you, and what you need to know about yourself to make decisions about the relationship.

Who's on Top?

After formulating the question, you next select which one of two decks represents each of you.

Pay attention to how the two of you arrive at this selection. Does one of you make the decision for both of you? How does your partner attempt to influence or change your decision?

Would you really like a certain deck, but acquiesce to your partner's decision? If your partner were absent, would you assign the decks differently?

Answering these questions may tell you about your position or role in the relationship and in the question at hand. Do they suggest one of you is more influential in your decision-making process than the other? Does the situation change as the reading progresses?

In writing about ways that inner aspects of our personalities battle one another, the late psychiatrist Fritz Perls coined the phrases "topdog" and "underdog."[80] Although topdog may make the initial decision, underdog usually wins by sabotaging that decision. Does this happen in your interactions together, or in your relationship with yourself?

If you are doing a solo reading, trust your intuition to tell you which deck to choose for you and which for the absent other. Before you proceed with the reading, however, you might pause and ask yourself what this choice says about your relationship. For instance, does choosing the larger deck for the other person show that you defer to the other, or believe he or she has more power in the relationship? Or even, do you wish he or she were stronger in the relationship?

Does choosing the larger deck for yourself show you believe you are the more powerful one in the relationship, or just wish you were? Would you select differently if your partner were present for the reading?

What do *you* think you are saying about yourself, the other person, and your relationship by assigning the decks the way you do? Always let your intuition make the selection first before you ask questions about the meaning of your choices.

---

[80] *Gestalt Therapy Verbatim*, 1969.

Chapter 11

Heartprints: Tarot for Two Layout Positions

When you understand the meaning of each card and each pair of cards, fitting that information into the heartprints of the Tarotscape adds another dimension to your understanding of your interaction with another.

It's a little like fitting together all the sky pieces of a picture puzzle, or all the meadow pieces, and then discovering where that nugget of color fits within the border.

In this chapter we introduce the 11 heartprint positions in the Tarot for Two Tarotscape. Following each description and commentary, we include questions which help you elicit maximum information from the cards and which stimulate conversation.

Why not work along with us? Pause to devise your question and assign your decks. Then lay down your cards in the appropriate order and heartprint. Have a notepad ready to jot down ideas as you read through each heartprint.

While many single Tarot layouts have you select or draw a card to act as significator (representing you), the selection of the decks in the Tarot for Two takes the place of a significator. Therefore, rather than having the significator as the first card laid down, the first card you draw for each deck is placed directly into the Tarot for Two first heartprint or Where am I? position.

The Cross:

WHERE AM I?

(Cards 1 and 2)

"Where am I? What am I doing here?" If you're like us, these are the first questions you ask when you realize you're in a problem situation.

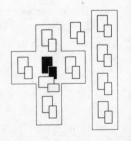

It's that time when you come out of a daze, or a denial, and wake up to the fact that something is not going right.

Or, if your question does not reflect a problem, but rather an issue you want to explore, Where am I? cards are the first step in determining where you stand presently. If you don't know where you are, it's hard to find out where you're going.

In traditional layouts, the first position is frequently called You-Here-Now. In the Tarot for Two, the first pair of cards reflect your present mental, emotional, and physical conditions. They provide information about the energies, attitudes, opinions, and outlooks related to the question which each of you brings to the reading.

Compare the cards, looking for clues to the role you both have played in creating the problem and for the resources each may be able to contribute to a possible solution.

1. If there are people on the cards, what is their status, age, sex, activity? Do you think they represent you or others involved in the question?

2. If there are no people, what do the animals (if any), or objects, on the cards indicate as prominent in your mind at present? Use Chapter 8 symbology to check whether they represent action or introspection, cooperation or isolation, loving or hostile feelings.

3. What do the people, animals, objects, or activities suggest about the attitudes, opinions, and expectations you are bringing into the current situation?

4. What do the cards suggest about your respective levels of mental functioning, including education and life experience, and their compatibility, or incompatibility, for your interaction?

5. What strengths or limitations that affect the question does each of you bring to the relationship?

6. What do the cards suggest about your sexual activities?

WHAT'S IN MY WAY?

(Cards 3 and 4)

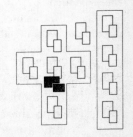

Often called the "crossing card" in traditional layouts, the pair of cards in this heartprint are thought of as signifying challenges. They show issues you need to deal with: problems, obstacles, positive or negative influences which may affect the question.

They can also reveal opportunities for growth which you may have overlooked, or avoided, and which must be settled within the relationship before you can arrive at a successful conclusion to the question.

What's in my way? cards help pinpoint possible differences and conflicts. They also can affirm ideas and intuitions gleaned from the Where am I? cards. Compare your What's in my way? cards to your Where am I? cards to determine what each of you needs to do to improve the relationship.

1. What kind of problem is it? Is the nature of the challenge mental (Swords), emotional (Cups), physical (Pentacles), or intuitive/spiritual (Wands)? Is it archetypal (Major Arcana) or mundane (Minor Arcana)?

2. How do other people or outside influences shown on the cards seem to be helping or interfering?

3. What resources or support does each have to help the other in facing the challenge?

4. Compare the challenges. Do you each recognize and acknowledge your own challenge and that of the other?

WHERE HAVE I BEEN?

(Cards 5 and 6)

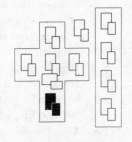

These cards reflect actual life experiences of each person, including attitudes, conditioning, what you have been taught by parents, and lessons you've learned or ignored. They also reveal patterns and connections from the past that affect the present question, including cultural backgrounds and work or career values.

Cards in this heartprint shed light on hidden—perhaps unspoken, possibly unrecognized—motives, drives, and fears. They show how these factors have brought you to this particular point of togetherness for growth in your lives.

Comparing Where have I been? and What's in my way? cards helps to determine how past experiences are related to the current challenge.

1. What do the cards show about the mental, intuitive/spiritual, emotional, or physical development each has experienced?

2. Do people, objects, and activities on the card point out shared or conflicting values?
3. What common experiences are shown?
4. Has the issue raised by the question come up before? Is there a repeating pattern here?
5. Does the presence of court cards reveal past experiences or attitudes about authority or leadership?
6. Do past sexual experiences influence the question?

WHAT'S BEEN HAPPENING?

(Cards 7 and 8)

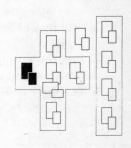

Cards here reflect events, situations, or behaviors (mental, physical or emotional) of the past one or two weeks—the recent past—which contribute to an awareness of the issue and the need to create a solution. This is "the straw that broke the camel's back."

Often these are the events that stimulated you to formulate the question or turn to the cards for a reading. Recent dreams sometimes come into awareness as you consider these cards.

1. Are your recent-past events of a mental, emotional, intuitive/ spiritual, or physical nature?
2. How do they differ between you?
3. Have recent-past events changed the mood of the relationship?
4. Has there been a shift in dominance or passivity of one or the other?
5. Has a recent sexual interaction influenced the issue?
6. Has a third party, or other influence, come into the picture?

WHAT'S IN STORE FOR ME?

(Cards 9 and 10)

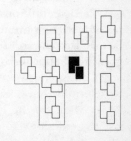

Issues that require attention or action are highlighted in these cards. They suggest a possible occurrence, within one or two weeks, that may stimulate a solution, or a crisis, unless changes are made.

Like the fairy tale that begins "Once upon a time," What's in store for me? cards show the next step in the sequence of events that started in the Where have I been? time, continues to be reflected in What's been happening? time, and is shaped by your Where am I? cards. Cards in this heartprint offer the first chance to see the possible results of that three-way sequence.

They may also show how each of you will handle soon-to-be events and, if you handle them that way, what effect your actions will have on the question.

1. Will your near-future events be of a mental, intuitive/spiritual, emotional, or physical nature?
2. Will they be caused by an outside influence or by one or both of you?
3. Will you respond actively or passively?
4. Which of you will be most affected by the events?
5. Are these expected events, or is there a surprise in store for one or both of you?

WHAT ARE MY OPTIONS?

(Cards 11 and 12)

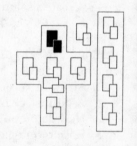

Reflecting the unfolding potential of all the cross cards, What are my options? cards may be the first opportunity you have to consider a new message or idea. They indicate possible direc-
tions and opportunities to consider in order to resolve "challenging" attitudes, or counteract prior conditioning. They also suggest potential effects of your joint work on the question and show what it might take for you and your partner to create a successful relationship.

1. Is the direction or opportunity of a mental, emotional, intuitive/spiritual or physical nature?
2. Do people on the cards indicate a shift in active/passive attitudes?
3. Are new avenues for growth shown?
4. Do the cards suggest possibilities for resolving any sexual conflict, if appropriate?

The Staff

WHO DO I THINK I AM?

(Cards 13 and 14)

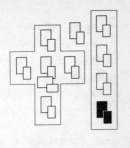

Not only do the cards in this heartprint reflect how we see ourselves and how we show ourselves to the public, or to our partner, but they can also reveal the basic inner nature behind the masks we present to the world. Depending on your philosophical stance, Who do I think I am? cards can also be considered to include karmic issues.

Included in our self-views can be our ideas about how we behave in given situations, the skills and limitations we recognize in ourselves, and the learnings we've stored from our life experiences. All these shape our subsequent perceptions and, therefore, the issue question.

1. What part does your self-view play in creating the question or situation?
2. Is your self-view consistent with your current behavior or your problem-solving approach?
3. How is each one's self-view, including sexual attitudes, similar to or different from the other's?

WHAT'S OUT THERE FOR ME?

(Cards 15 and 16)

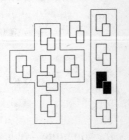

These cards suggest current environmental influences (people, places, things) that affect you and that also affect how you interact with your partner.

Influences, including events, that can in some way affect the question or situation may be identified. They may not necessarily be influences over which you have control, and can be either a help or a hindrance. On the other hand, they can also show what help is available from the environment for you to draw on.

1. Are there outside influences, communication, or information which can be utilized?
2. Are the influences shown on the cards common to both of you?
3. How will each person react to these influences?

4. Are confrontations or compromises indicated?

5. Are there other people to consider or who may intervene to help?

6. What emotional atmosphere do the symbols on the cards show?

7. Are there external factors that may influence sexual attitudes or behavior?

WHAT DO I EXPECT?

(Cards 17 and 18)

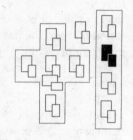

Identified expectations (hopes, fears, wants, and wishes), as well as unspoken expectations which influence the relationship and which need to be explored or resolved, are pinpointed through this heartprint question.

Your expectations may have resulted from past experiences or may have developed out of the present relationship. They may or may not be tied to your life goals or fantasies.

1. Do your expectations involve receiving, getting, doing, serving, or just being?

2. Are your individual expectations compatible or in conflict?

3. How do your expectations relate to the question?

4. Are sexual expectations influencing the question?

5. How do your expectations compare with your Where am I? cards?

WHERE DOES ALL THIS LEAD?

(Cards 19 and 20)

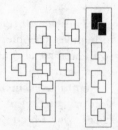

Sometimes called the outcome cards, cards in this heartprint have a special kinship with all the other cards in the spread.

They can be understood in a number of ways. At times they clearly represent the final outcome—the grand summation—of the reading and of all the cards in the Tarotscape, the answer to the question. They are like the final, conclusive, and satisfying stroke of your brush when your heart tells you that you are finished.

However, when these cards do not seem definitive, regard them as a "partial outcome." Combining their information with your What are my options? cards often answers the question or suggests new directions to consider.

In either case, reviewing the eight cards in the staff at this time reminds you what inner and outer support is available for you to draw upon.

1. What are the similarities or differences in your respective outcomes?
2. What skills or talents are available that you can use to resolve the question?
3. Are they of a mental, emotional, intuitive/spiritual or physical nature?
4. How do these skills or talents complement, or conflict, with each other?
5. How does the outcome compare with your expectations (What do I expect?)?

WHAT ELSE IS NEW?

(Cards 21 and 22)

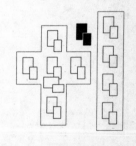

An optional position, this heartprint frequently reveals other influences or spiritual aspects you might want to consider. "Last thoughts," or ideas needing further attention or inquiry, are often revealed here.

Sometimes they show additional or potential resources available to you. They may also yield a question or a point of departure for a future reading.

Blending information from your What else is new? cards with that from What are my options? and Where does all this lead? can sometimes offer additional suggestions for the resolution of your question.

1. Does the information on the cards suggest additional resources for implementing the outcome?
2. What emotional, spiritual, or sexual growth possibilities are shown in your What else is new? cards?

Keeping Track of Tarot for Two Readings

If you laid out a set of cards as you worked through the questions in this chapter, you may want to record your layout on a Tarotscape form similar to the sample shown on the next page.

Date _____

P1 _Woman_

P2 _Man_

Question _How can my_
boyfriend and I make
better use of our time
together?

Queen of Cups
| 19 |
| 20 |
Eight of Wands
Where does all this lead?

The Hierophant
| 17 |
| 18 |
Ten of Swords
What do I expect?

Seven of Swords
| 15 |
| 16 |
Three of Swords
What's out there for me?

The Devil
| 13 |
| 14 |
Nine of Wands
Who do I think I am?

The Fool
| 21 |
| 22 |
Queen of Wands
What else is new?

Ten of Cups
| 11 |
| 12 |
Temperance
What are my options?
Where am I?

| 1 |
Nine of Swords
The Empress
| 2 |
| 3 |
Knight of Pentacles
| 4 |
Six of Cups
What's in my way?

What's in store
for me?
| 9 |
Ace of Cups
| 10 |
Justice

Three of Wands
| 5 |
| 6 |
Nine of Swords
Where have I been?

What's been
happening?
| 7 |
Page of Cups
| 8 |
Four of Swords

TAROTSCAPE

The Tarot for Two Tarotscape form lets you keep a concise picture of each of your readings. Its continued use provides you with ongoing records of your Tarotscapes, and the progress in your relationships.

Simply write the names of the cards in the appropriate spaces as you turn them over during readings or when summarizing a completed reading. In our sample Tarotscape, the card names are in bold type for ease in distinguishing them. Naturally, yours will be written in pencil or ink.

You might want separate sections in your notebook for each type of relationship you explore with Tarot for Two: work, family, romance, projects, your inner child, your higher self, and your deity.

By reflecting cards which you draw regularly, a series of Tarotscapes highlight continuing characteristics or resources within one relationship or across several.

A blank Tarotscape form suitable for reproduction is included in Appendix 1.

The Heart of the Matter

The first two cards in a single-deck reading and the first four cards of the Tarot for Two are called the micro-cross. Rachel Pollack[81] believes information gleaned from the micro-cross often contains the kernel of the entire issue. Cards drawn for the remainder of the heartprints then merely amplify the micro-cross framework.

Where am I? cards show your states of inner being and the way those can help you face challenges and take action in daily life. They present both the resources and the hang-ups—in the form of attitudes, opinions, views, skills, previous conditioning—each of you has when the reading begins.

What's in my way? cards uncover your challenges, the hurdles you will need to overcome before you can successfully resolve your question.

For us—today's heroes and heroines—challenges no longer come in the exact shape of dragons. But they do come in many other fire-breathing shapes, sizes, and disguises. Most simply, they reflect anything that calls out for attention or requires effort.

Altogether the four cards of the micro-cross create a working hypothesis to be fleshed out by the other cards in the Tarotscape. Meeting the challenge from our Tarot for Two reading requires us to fully use

---

[81] *Seventy-Eight Degrees of Wisdom*, Part 2, 1983.

the abilities, energies, or resources spelled out in the remainder of the Tarotscape.

Begin analyzing your four micro-cross cards by considering the *suits* and the *qualities* they reflect: (1) intuitive/spiritual (Wands and Major Arcana), (2) intellectual (Swords), (3) emotional (Cups), and (4) physical or material aspects (Pentacles).

These suit qualities—some readers think of them as energies—are your first clue to personality aspects which, by their presence or absence, you may be over- or underutilizing.

For instance, in the sample Tarotscape shown on page 180 (drawn by one of our students and discussed in more detail in Appendices 3 and 4), the card drawn for the woman in the Where am I? heartprint is the Nine of Swords, and for her boyfriend, The Empress, Major Arcana III. She comes into the situation actively expressing her intellectual qualities, while he enters actively expressing his intuitive/spiritual qualities.

Her challenge card (Knight of Pentacles) suggests she needs to attend in some way to the physical or material aspects. His challenge card (Six of Cups) shows he needs to pay attention to the emotional plane. Because all four qualities are represented in the micro-cross, the potential for balance exists if both attend to the relationship challenge rather than avoid it.

The mode and action of the micro-cross challenge are established through the card meanings and numerological symbology. Her Knight (12; also 1 + 2 = 3) of Pentacles:

- gives direction (knights)
- is materialistic and practical (meanings for Knight of Pentacles)
- suggests completion; fruits of a partnership (the number 3); fruition and manifestation (the number 12).

So, for success, her challenge is to give practical directions related to the physical or material aspects of the relationship.

His Six of Cups suggests:

- reconciliation; harmony; childhood memories (meanings for Six of Cups)
- harmony of opposites; success; reconciliation (the number 6).

His challenge is to resolve the discrepancies between his intuitive process (probably influenced by childhood memories) and his emotions.

When the suits in your *individual* micro-cross are different, part of the challenge involves working toward bringing the What's in my way?

quality—intuitive/spiritual, intellectual, emotional, or physical—into the relationship.

Two cards of the same suit in an individual micro-cross suggest an excess of that suit's quality. Depending on the card meaning and its numerological value, most likely the challenge will be to reduce it.

If the What's in my way? card is a so-called negative card, it may be highlighting a belief which actively shapes present perceptions and behavior.

As your reading progresses, keep checking subsequent cards with the micro-cross hypothesis. They may show how the micro-cross situation came about and what additional resources you have to meet your challenge.

Chapter 12

Putting It All Together

Reader as Healer

Throughout history the element of disruption, whether psychological or societal, has been implicit in the notion of witchcraft.

Often we feel the need for a Tarot for Two reading because we, too, are "bewitched," in the sense that something has been disrupted. Something is not quite working within the relationship; something puzzles us.

In a mythological sense, when we do a Tarot reading—especially for another—we act as restorers. Drawing upon some combination of intuitive, psychic, and learned skills, we re-create a timeless healing ceremony quite similar to those enacted by medicine men, shamans, and South American *curanderos*.

Even though the shaman waits for revelations from the gods or spirits, he has been trained to make sense of this gift when it arrives.

Like the medicine man's, your skill comes into play through:

1. knowledge of card meanings
2. knowledge of Tarot for Two heartprints
3. a well-honed ability to translate Tarot language (symbols, images, numbers, colors, etc.) into understandable ideas
4. opening your intuition and impressions for selecting significant factors, what Murry Hope calls tuning in to the "cosmic shorthand."[82]

If you need help in sharpening your intuitive impressions, consider the tapes by Thomas Condon[83] and the exercises by Craig Junjulas.[84]

The Developing Scene

After you—or you and a partner—are clear about your question and which deck represents each of you, shuffle and cut your decks, holding your question in mind. If you are reading alone, shuffle and cut your

---

[82] *Practical Techniques of Psychic Self-Defense*, 1983.
[83] *Expanded Intuition Training*. Workbook and six cassette tapes, 1987.
[84] *Psychic Tarot*, 1985.

deck first. Then shuffle and cut the second deck, mentally asking higher powers or your higher self for guidance to assist you in representing the absent person.

If you are reading for a friend and the third person is not present, let your friend shuffle and cut his or her own representative deck. You shuffle and cut the deck for the absent one, also asking for guidance that the cards represent that person.[85]

Turn, place, and interpret the cards one heartprint at a time, allowing the unfolding story to take place.

When you grasp the information that can be gained from each heartprint, are familiar with the card meanings, and understand the processes of the worksheets in Chapter 13, you are ready to do actual readings rather than practice readings. When that time comes, we suggest you work first with someone who is also learning the Tarot, or with an understanding friend.

Always approach your reading with an open mind about what may be revealed through the cards. When you are reading for another, translate the language of the cards without making value judgments about it.

In a Tarot for Two reading, the Tarotscape becomes clear only as additional cards are laid out, just as the sense of any painting becomes more evident when you add more objects, colors, and subtle shading.

Earlier we suggested that the carefully formed question acted as and defined the border of a picture puzzle. To place the first piece within that border, turn over the larger (bottom) card first and read from that.

When you are reading with another person present, each of you should focus on the question as you turn over your respective cards.

After each card is turned, state aloud

a. what the heartprint is

b. what the card is.

For instance, "This is the Where am I? heartprint, and the card representing me [or the absent person] is the Two of Pentacles."

Then state

a. the meaning of the heartprint

b. the action taking place on the card.

"The Where am I? heartprint shows the energies or feelings I have about the question. Here a person balances two pentacles."

Relate the action on the card to you. "I am balancing two different ideas or issues, and my energy is being divided between them."

---

[85]Professional Tarot readers develop their own special ways of shuffling, cutting, and dealing decks. If you have not already developed your own style, you may want to consult the section titled "It's All in the Wrist," Chapter 6.

Think of each card as a piece of the puzzle which eventually will bring the developing scene into focus. If any person on your card is not the same sex as you, consider whether the figure could represent the other person in the relationship, a relative, close friend, neighbor, co-worker, or boss. If none apply, the card figure may represent an attitude or quality you have—such as fear, happiness, strength, caution, greed, etc.—or an inner aspect of yourself. For instance, if you are a woman, could the male figure on the card represent your masculine side? Could a female figure represent the feminine aspects of the man in the relationship?

If the people or objects on the cards do not seem to relate to the question, read another element, such as colors or mood depicted.

Pay attention first to the obvious meaning of the card and to your reaction. Honor and respect your first impression. Then look to other factors on the card to supplement and clarify the general meaning.

The Dynamic Duo

When you understand the first card in each heartprint, turn up the second card for that heartprint and translate its message. Then, having read both cards separately, compare them for an image of your interaction.

Just as your separate cards tap into individual attitudes and experiences, heartprint pairs illustrate areas of compatibility or friction—the dynamics of the relationship.

For each heartprint duo, look for:

1. strong points, similarities, and dissimilarities (as revealed by background, foreground, people, numbers, action, suits)
2. conflicts or obstacles to your interaction which you may not have previously recognized or acknowledged
3. patterns of behavior, outlooks, or approaches to problem solving
4. whether the cards indicate one of you has greater power, dominance, or influence over the other, and if you agree with the cards about this
5. areas of communication that have been ignored or are missing
6. changing balances or imbalances in the relationship.

Continually look for a theme, story, or pattern from the unfolding cards. At times it may point to a need to restate the question, or it may lead you to recognize a different aspect of the issue.

And the Winners Are . . .

All the cards and heartprints tap into information that leads toward resolving the question. Your task is to translate the Tarot's symbolic messages into actions for you to consider.

We believe that on some level most of us already know, or have clues to, the answers to our questions. The Tarot for Two reading gently nudges your intuition and stimulates you to consider alternatives and/ or to see your situation from a different perspective. It helps you learn to tune in to your inner wisdom for assistance.

In more ways than one, interpreting Tarotscapes is like learning to understand hieroglyphic writing. On the first level, there is simply learning to understand the components of the hieroglyph in order to be able to translate it. You develop your first-level skills by:

1. practicing Worksheet #1 (Chapter 13) until you are able to do the process mentally during a reading
2. answering the heartprint questions following the heartprint descriptions in Chapter 11.

When you have completed one or both of these processes, you should be able to state at least one simple and direct answer to your question.

However, just as trained anthropologists understand that, taken together, hieroglyphs spell out an action or a scene, you probably already have recognized that, in fact, your question can be answered in more than one way.

As you become more skilled at reading the cards—or strive to answer more complex questions—your answer may take the form: "This is what I/we can do to accomplish our goals . . . " Or, "Here are some options and choices we have for tackling the issue . . . "

Attending to heartstyles (Worksheet #2) and power patterns (Worksheet #3) is a way to move into second-level understanding of the issue and to explore additional alternatives. The Where am I?/Where have I been? heartstyle gives the present-time information about the question. The Where have I been?/What's been happening? combination shows past behaviors or beliefs that modify the present behavior. What are my options? cards take all that went before and suggest a possible new direction. The staff cards highlight the inner and outer forces available to draw upon in resolving the question or situation.

Using any one or more combinations of these methods to expand your outlook and perceive alternative pathways opens the channel for transformation. To recognize possible options—even if you decide to make no change—means that for at least one therapeutic moment your Tarotscape granted you access to an unprecedented vista.

Chapter 13

Sharpening Your Perspective

Like perspective lines used in drawings to provide reference points for the spacing and proportion of buildings and other structures, the worksheets in this chapter provide a reliable record—a different type of reference point—of the development of both your Tarot and your relationship artistries.

Please feel free to duplicate the blank copies in this chapter to help you expand your Tarot for Two skills.

Tarot Trainers

If you had a tricycle as a child, perhaps you remember when you outgrew it and became ready for your first bicycle. The progress from three wheels to two is a rite of passage of sorts. There is an element of pride ("I've grown up enough to be ready for this") and sometimes a little fear ("Gulp. Two wheels instead of three"). Sometimes parents put training wheels on the bicycle to make the transition easier and to reduce scrapes and bumps.

The worksheets in the remainder of this chapter are our set of training wheels. They offer a second way for you to master the Tarot for Two.

Using them fosters in-depth comprehension of the Tarot for Two interpretive process. Accessing the kind of information they guide you toward is what a skilled Tarot reader does in his or her head during a reading.

Using the worksheets, at least in the beginning, helps you gain confidence in your interpretive skills, sharpen your insights, and develop a mental process which you can count on. When you can do the entire comparison-interpretation-summarization process mentally, you will have graduated to a "two-wheeler." Like the bike rider who lets his body automatically make appropriate shifts in balance, you will rely on your now-trained intuitive skills for selecting appropriate information.

If you want to begin exploring the Tarot for Two by using the worksheets alone, imagine yourself and another as having a question. Shuffle and deal two decks into the format of the Tarot for Two and complete the worksheets as instructed in this chapter.

If you created a layout while working through the heartprints in Chapter 11, you certainly can use that Tarotscape.

Alternatively, Appendix 4 contains a Tarot for Two interpretation completed by one of our students, using the worksheets only. That Tarotscape is shown at the end of Chapter 11 and again in Appendix 4. You might wish to use it as the basis for filling out the worksheets in this chapter.

If so, when you have completed your worksheets, compare them with those in the example worksheets in Appendix 4. Notice where yours differ. This does not mean your responses are wrong or incorrect. Rather, comparing your responses with those of another person, who undoubtedly attends to different aspects of the cards, helps you pinpoint strengths and possible gaps in your perceptions.

If you begin by working on your personal issues with another, or if you and a friend are learning the Tarot for Two together, take time to complete the worksheets during your practice readings so you get the most comprehensive and accurate interpretation possible.

The Heartbeat of the Relationship

(Worksheet #1)

By a progression of steps, the first worksheet leads you from the separate card meanings into an understanding of the various ideas or attitudes—we call them stances—each person has about the issue. Then it links the 22 card meanings and the 22 individual stance statements into 11 interpretive statements—heartlinks—which summarize your interaction as a couple.

Heartlinks constitute the active forces and resources you have available to resolve the issue. Taken together, the 11 heartlinks are like the colors in a painting. Too much of one color can overshadow the others. Improperly blended, they become a dull and muddy mixture. Properly mixed and put on the canvas with a good idea and the right perspective, they result in a Rembrandt.

Likewise, none of the individual forces and resources in your relationships are totally good or necessarily harmful in themselves. Just as for the successful artist, it is in combining them with both inspiration and discipline that you achieve your relationship masterpiece.

Exercise 12—Using Worksheet #1
The Heartbeat of the Relationship

1. Enter the names of the people or projects you want information about, designating Person 1 as the person or project using the larger deck and Person 2 as the person represented by the smaller deck.

2. Write the date and your question in the appropriate spaces.

3. After you turn over the larger (bottom) card for a given heartprint (position), write its name in the card's P1 blank.

Keeping the question in mind, write a brief meaning in column 1 (Meanings), either from memory or by consulting the meanings in Chapters 3 and 4.

4. Repeat for the top (smaller) card from the second deck, writing its name in the card's P2 blank and its meaning in column 1.

5. Consider the card meanings and the heartprint descriptions (see Chapter 11) for each pair of cards. Combine them into a short statement that reflects your understanding of each person's behavior or approach—their stance in the world, so to speak—with respect to the initial question.

Write this statement in the Stances column. (Note: When you finish the worksheet, you will have 22 stance statements.)

Remember, in creating stance statements, you are integrating your understanding of the pair of card meanings and the heartprint description and asking yourself how this information relates to the question.

More information on how to create stance statements follows Worksheet 1.

6. Draw cards for the second heartprint and enter in the same way.

7. Following the first two heartprints, insert the micro-cross statement. (See Chapter 11, "The Heart of the Matter" section, for directions for the micro-cross.)

8. Continue the process of turning over two cards for each heartprint and writing meanings and stance statements for each pair until you have completed the layout.

9. Consider how the stance statements for each heartprint supply information toward answering your question.

Combine them into a single statement (heartlink) for each heartprint which describes your interaction as a couple. It summarizes the link between the two of you and your issue.

Enter one statement in the Heartlink column for each position. You will have 11 heartlink statements.

More information on how to create heartlinks follows this worksheet.

10. At this point you should be able to list some insights you now have about the nature of the issue or problem and be able to write one or more plans of action to pursue.

Worksheet #1

The Heartbeat of the Relationship

Person 1 _____

Person 2 _____

Date _____

Question _____

_____

WHERE AM I?

    Cards: P1_____   P2 _____

        Meanings   *Stances*   *Heartlink*

  1. _____ _____ _____

       _____ _____ _____

  2. _____ _____ _____

       _____ _____ _____

WHAT'S IN MY WAY?

    Cards: P1_____   P2 _____

        Meanings   *Stances*   *Heartlink*

  3. _____ _____ _____

       _____ _____ _____

  4. _____ _____ _____

       _____ _____ _____

Worksheet #1 (cont.)

Micro-Cross Statement

_____

_____

_____

_____

WHERE HAVE I BEEN?

Cards: P1_____ P2 _____

Meanings	Stances	Heartlink
5. _____	_____	_____
_____	_____	_____
6. _____	_____	_____
_____	_____	_____

WHAT'S BEEN HAPPENING?

Cards: P1_____ P2 _____

Meanings	Stances	Heartlink
7. _____	_____	_____
_____	_____	_____
8. _____	_____	_____
_____	_____	_____

Worksheet #1 (cont.)

WHAT'S IN STORE FOR ME?

Cards: P1_____ P2 _____

	Meanings	*Stances*	*Heartlink*
9.	_____	_____	_____
	_____	_____	_____
10.	_____	_____	_____
	_____	_____	_____

WHAT ARE MY OPTIONS?

Cards: P1_____ P2 _____

	Meanings	*Stances*	*Heartlink*
11.	_____	_____	_____
	_____	_____	_____
12.	_____	_____	_____
	_____	_____	_____

WHO DO I THINK I AM?

Cards: P1_____ P2 _____

	Meanings	*Stances*	*Heartlink*
13.	_____	_____	_____
	_____	_____	_____

Worksheet #1 (cont.)

	Meanings	**Stances**	**Heartlink**
14.	_____	_____	_____
	_____	_____	_____

WHAT'S OUT THERE FOR ME?

Cards: P1 _____ P2 _____

	Meanings	**Stances**	**Heartlink**
15.	_____	_____	_____
	_____	_____	_____
16.	_____	_____	_____
	_____	_____	_____

WHAT DO I EXPECT?

Cards: P1 _____ P2 _____

	Meanings	**Stances**	**Heartlink**
17.	_____	_____	_____
	_____	_____	_____
18.	_____	_____	_____
	_____	_____	_____

Worksheet #1 (cont.)

WHERE DOES ALL THIS LEAD?

Cards: P1_____   P2_____

       Meanings   *Stances*   *Heartlink*

19. _____   _____   _____

    _____   _____   _____

20. _____   _____   _____

    _____   _____   _____

WHAT ELSE IS NEW?

Cards: P1_____   P2_____

       Meanings   *Stances*   *Heartlink*

21. _____   _____   _____

    _____   _____   _____

22. _____   _____   _____

    _____   _____   _____

       Insights   *Plan(s) of Action*

_____   _____

_____   _____

_____   _____

_____   _____

The information entered in the Meanings column of Worksheet #1 is rather concrete and definite. Stance statements derive from those meanings, but they are your opportunity to get a little psychological and figure out what's happening between this pair. Here is where you translate the meanings of card elements into personal terms.

Stance statements say how a person behaves or communicates. They summarize a person's mental or physical responses to what he or she encounters. They suggest attitudes. They help identify emotional options or resources a person has available to handle the problem.

Often we can infer an attitude from cards drawn, combined with what we know about a person's behavior. For example, in the exercise in Chapter 14, the man draws the Ace of Wands for the Where am I? position. That, combined with the fact that he has come with the woman to the reading, lets us conclude he has an attitude of readiness toward resolving the situation. He intuitively (Wands) is open to a new direction.

The Hierophant has been drawn several times in the sample readings included in this book. In general, The Hierophant indicates a time for teaching or learning (the teacher will appear), or attending to higher values (spiritual, moral, or religious). Its more base meanings include exerting or experiencing peer pressure and a need to conform.

Below are the various stances created based on the querents' question and the heartprint where The Hierophant appeared:

Question	Heartprint	Stance
What is the matter with our communication? (Chapter 14)	What's in store for me?	She will be open to her intuition.
What do my garden and I need from one another? (Chapter 15)	What's in store for me?	You want to know what will make the garden happy.
How can my boyfriend and I make better use of our time together? (Appendix 4)	What do I expect?	She knows she can count on her faith and inner wisdom.

Would you agree with these stance statements? What alternative stance statements would you make?

When you have your 22 stance statements (two stances for each pair of cards), you are ready to create heartlink statements. Ask yourself, "What does this pair of cards in this position tell me about how this couple interacts with respect to their question?"

Or, "If two people made these stance statements about themselves to me, what do I think this says about, or for, their life as a couple?"

The 11 heartlink statements show how your interactions contribute to, or create, your problem. They also indicate the resources or talents the two of you have available to change those interactions and resolve the issue.

Heartlinks may be written as a feeling, an idea, an awareness or insight, a way of behaving, or a possibility. They are couched in present, past, or future terms, depending on the heartprint in which they appear.

Consider how the stance pairs express balance or imbalance in the relationship. Look for contrasting or complementary stances, areas of agreement and of conflict. How is this couple facing or avoiding certain issues? What do their stances show about their available strengths, gaps, and resources?

It is tricky to step out of your own preconceptions or desires and create the heartlink statements for yourself. If you are learning the Tarot for Two with someone else, it might be easier to create one another's heartlinks. If not, pretend you are an outside observer trying to determine how two stance statements link to spell out something the couple is doing, needs to be doing, or needs to consider.

It is sometimes helpful—or at least gives you a little distance from yourself—to pretend that an acquaintance has told you that when he asked two people to answer the question "Where am I?" for instance, he discovered something about each (stances). Now your acquaintance is asking you to make sense out of that couple's interaction, or potential interaction, using those two sentences.

If you need additional ideas, review the examples of heartlink statements in the completed worksheets in Chapters 14 and 15 and Appendix 4.

Worksheet #1 may supply you with enough information to suggest new ideas or plans of action to try. What remains to be done cannot be accomplished by worksheet. Now you need to consider whether the new viewpoint or possible new direction "answers" your question, or gives you a new hunch about it. And you need to consider whether you want to, or are willing to, work through those issues at this time in your life and your relationship.

For instance, the reading in Chapter 16 indicates that Nan would develop certain aspects of herself if she entered into the relationship she and Betty were considering. Nan decided, however, that, given other factors in the reading, that particular growth was not something she wanted to accomplish through a working collaboration with Betty.

Heartstyles
(Worksheet #2)

If Worksheet #1 does not provide you with enough new insights—your "a*ha*" experience—or if you want additional information, use Worksheet #2, which simplifies an advanced Tarot reading technique.

In an actual Tarot reading, once a reader explains the card and position meanings for you, she may analyze the interrelationship between cards in one or more positions. Tarot readers often refer to these as "correspondences."

Because they shed additional light on your interaction, we call them heartstyles and have selected five combinations that shed special light on the dynamics of your relationship. Use Worksheet #2 to learn to spot their interaction and significance.

Exercise 13—Using Worksheet #2
Heartstyles
To begin, simply transfer the heartlink statements from Worksheet #1 into the second column of Worksheet #2 in the heartprint combinations indicated. This prepares you to analyze their interrelationship.

Create a sentence or phrase that shows both persons' roles in creating the problem, as well as resources they have to draw on. Enter that statement in the Heartstyle column.

Explanations of each of the five combinations follow Worksheet #2.

WHERE AM I?/WHERE HAVE I BEEN? HEART-STYLE: Comparing Where have I been? to Where am I? cards shows whether your current mind-sets are long-standing viewpoints or derive

Worksheet #2

Heartstyles

Person 1 _____   Person 2 _____

Question _____   Date _____

Heartprints	*Heartlinks*	*Heartstyle*
Where am I?	_____	_____
	_____	_____
Where have I been?	_____	_____
	_____	Current or long-standing viewpoints
	*	*
Where have I been?	_____	_____
	_____	_____
What's been happening?	_____	_____
	_____	Possible changes affecting the interaction
	*	*
What's in my way?	_____	_____
	_____	_____

Worksheet #2 (cont.)

Heartprints	**Heartlinks**	**Heartstyle**
What's in store for me?	_____	_____
	_____	_____
	_____	
		Effects of acceptance or rejection of challenges
	*	*
Where am I?	_____	_____
	_____	_____
Who do I think I am?	_____	_____
	_____	
		How outer behavior conforms to inner belief
	*	*
What are my options?	_____	_____
	_____	_____
What do I expect?	_____	_____
	_____	
		Are expectations realistic for unfolding potential?
	*	*

from recent developments. Together they shed light on old patterns or old traumas you may have transferred onto the present issue. This is especially true if the two cards are of the same suit, the same numerical value of different suits, or show the same action.

WHERE HAVE I BEEN?/WHAT'S BEEN HAPPENING?: The comparison between What's been happening? and Where have I been? suggests possible changes in established patterns which affect your interaction: a crisis, a change of direction, perhaps. Or they may shed light on aspects of an ongoing situation that have been ignored. They pinpoint causal or motivational factors creating discontent, anxiety, or the need for the reading.

WHAT'S IN MY WAY?/WHAT'S IN STORE FOR ME?: The effect of your decision to accept or reject the challenges in the Tarotscape may be revealed by comparing What's in store for me? and What's in my way? cards. They also show abilities or resources that may open up for you to help you meet your challenges, or the consequences of making no change.

WHERE AM I?/WHO DO I THINK I AM?: How your observable behaviors conform to your inner beliefs about yourself is revealed by this comparison. Sometimes it addresses the differences between our hidden, private self (Who do I think I am?) and our public self, what we show to the world (Where am I?). If there is a discrepancy between outer and inner, consider how you could make them more alike, bringing about congruency. Observe whether your Who do I think I am? situation supports or sabotages your Where am I? situation.

WHAT ARE MY OPTIONS?/WHAT DO I EXPECT?: Comparing these two heartprints—What do I expect? and What are my options?—guides you to consider whether your joint expectations enhance or interfere with your mutual options. They give you a sense of whether your expectations are realistic. They offer you the opportunity to identify whether your separate expectations and options are compatible and, if not, whether it's time to negotiate rather than manipulate.

For examples of heartstyle statements, see the completed worksheets in Chapters 14 and 15 and Appendix 4. Heartstyle statements give you the opportunity to compare summaries of both querents' skills or talents (heartlink) for two heartprint positions. They help you decide where this couple is, i.e., what conflicts they may experience or need to resolve, what resources they have to draw on, what possibilities exist—in short, what they need to be aware of to reach their goal.

Power Patterns
(Worksheet #3)

Certain card patterns or combinations appearing in a spread indicate a strong focus of your efforts or energies, an emotional wallop. They direct attention to an ongoing process between or within each person so important it must be acknowledged.

> ### Exercise 14—Using Worksheet #3
> ### Power Patterns
> For this exercise, refer to your completed Tarot for Two Tarotscape form.
>
> Tally the number of cards for each person according to the categories shown. In the Pattern Interpretation column, write a brief interpretation, using the guidelines that follow.

Major Arcana:

This section is completed only if one person has three or more Major Arcana cards in his or her spread. That person brings a strong introspective focus to the situation and may have to confront and deal with deep-seated drives or habitual ways of interacting to bring about change. This pattern can also highlight an issue which has reached such a pitch that it can no longer be ignored.

If one person has three or more Major Arcana while the other has two or less, it is likely that the person with more Major Arcana has more invested in the issue, or in the resolution of the question. Often this indicates an entrenched position fortified by heavy emotion. It may be easier for the person with the majority of Minor Arcana cards to compromise or to see alternatives, so at least consider his or her ideas.

Court Cards:

Having three or more court cards shows that other people are contributing to or influencing the issue, and their roles and purposes need to be clarified.

The specific court cards may help you decide who these people are. If you are able to, tentatively identify them, clarify what you think their roles are, and verify it with them, perhaps later, if possible. For Kings and Queens, consider male and female authority figures such as parents, teachers, bosses. Pages may represent a young man or woman who brings

Worksheet #3

Power Patterns

Person 1 _____ Person 2 _____

Question _____ Date _____

	Tally	*Pattern Interpretation*
1. Major Arcana	P-1 ___	_____
	P-2 ___	_____
2. Court Cards	P-1 ___	_____
	P-2 ___	_____
3. Suits		
Wands	P-1 ___	_____
	P-2 ___	_____
Cups	P-1 ___	_____
	P-2 ___	_____
Swords	P-1 ___	_____
	P-2 ___	_____
Pentacles	P-1 ___	_____
	P-2 ___	_____
4. Duplicate Numbers	P-1 ___	_____
	P-2 ___	_____
5. Duplicate Cards	P-1 ___	_____
	P-2 ___	_____

you information in some form (a gossip, a confidant), or urges you to consider other ideas and possibilities. Knights suggest someone who may be urging you to take action, perhaps of a courageous nature, but on the other hand, it can also be hasty or ill-advised.

Alternatively, if you are unable to identify anyone in your two lives who is involved with you in these behaviors, consider the court cards as messages from these various aspects of yourself.

Suits:

Three cards or more in the same suit emphasize the qualities (see Chapter 4) of that suit. A missing suit shows an aspect of your life, or of the question, that you need to attend to. When the same suit is missing for both persons, you both need to take definitive action to bring that quality into your relationship.

Duplicate Numbers:

When three or more of the same number (three sixes, three fives) appear for one or both persons, pay special attention to the numerological symbolism of those cards (see Chapter 8).

Duplicate Cards:

Duplicate cards (two Temperance cards, two Ten of Pentacles) anywhere in a Tarot for Two layout, and particularly in the same heartprint, show a shared approach, attitude, or behavior.

Examples of completed Power Patterns worksheets are in Chapter 14 and Appendix 4. After the initial tally is complete, work first to understand what's being expressed by the person with three or more cards in any of the categories. Then you should be able to determine what the person with less than three cards needs or is not expressing, or, perhaps, what the two people need to do to bring more balance into their relationship.

Part 5

Tarotscapes

Tarot Tutor 5

"Please, Lord, let me have a once-upon-a-time, once-in-a-lifetime soul-stirring adventure." That prayer, hidden in the psyches of most of us, makes myths and fairy tales, films and soap operas, everlastingly popular. It is a prayer challenging the tedium of trivia-filled days. It may even turn up in the guise of a Tarot for Two question.

"What is the matter with our communication?" was the dilemma of a couple who came for the Tarot for Two reading reflected in Chapter 14. Presented in worksheet form, Chapter 14 also offers you the opportunity to complete worksheets and compare your responses with those of the authors.

Chapter 15 shows how you can use the Tarot for Two to gain insight into a project. It also demonstrates the use of two quite different types of decks, in this case a serious (Rider-Waite) and a humorous (Morgan's "Du Wacky Du") pair.

An edited transcript (Chapter 16) of a joint reading by the authors highlights issues between two women considering a collaborative effort.

When you clear the clutter from your prayerful roadway, your Tarotscape answer may just pave the way for that once-in-a-lifetime relationship.

Chapter 14

What Is the Matter with Our Communication? (A Couple with a Problem—A Practice Opportunity)

Change the way a couple think and communicate and you change their lives, according to Dr. Aaron Beck, creator of cognitive therapy. In a 1988 interview with the *Los Angeles Times,* Beck, author of *Love Is Never Enough,* said that ingrained differences in the thinking and communicating styles of men and women are a big part of the problem in many relationships. Women display more listening skills and cues; men tend to remain silent and expressionless. When women can talk about problems, they perceive the relationship as working. Men think that if you have to talk about a problem, the relationship *isn't* working.[86]

With the couple who came for this reading, the husband's Where am I? card reveals that he wants to take the lead in communicating, but in his own way. His wife's underlying style of communicating is revealed in her What's in my way? card: she tries to make too big a deal out of every issue. The attitudes and behaviors revealed by their Tarotscape show the pitfalls in this couple's communication.

This chapter interprets a Tarot for Two reading using worksheet formats. It offers you an opportunity to check your insights with those of an experienced Tarot for Two reader.

Although we have shown the completed Tarotscape before presenting Exercise 15, in an actual reading you would see only one pair of cards at a time and have to make an interpretive statement. We suggest, therefore, that if you do Exercise 15, you write your meaning, stance and heartlink statements for each position without considering the cards that follow.

> **Exercise 15—What Is the Matter with Our Communication?:** *If you wish to use this sample reading as an exercise in practicing with the worksheets, duplicate one complete set of Worksheets #1–3. Have on hand two different-sized Rider-Waite decks.*

---

[86]Anne C. Roark, *Los Angeles Times,* November 29, 1988, Part V, pp 1, 3.

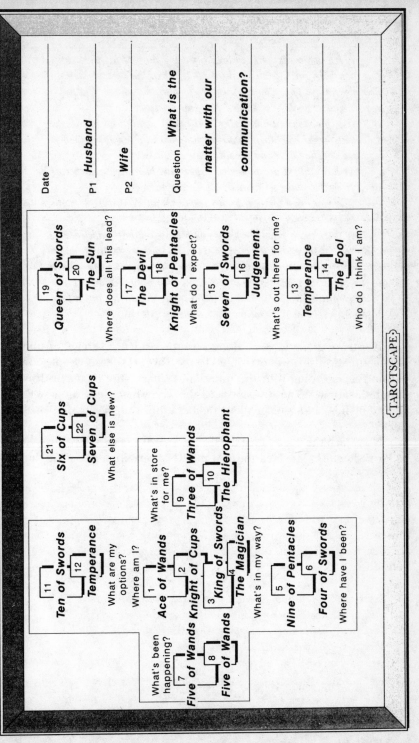

Date _____

P1 _Husband_

P2 _Wife_

Question ___What is the___ ___matter with our___ ___communication?___

19 **_Queen of Swords_**
20 **_The Sun_**
Where does all this lead?

17 **_The Devil_**
18 **_Knight of Pentacles_**
What do I expect?

15 **_Seven of Swords_**
16 **_Judgement_**
What's out there for me?

13 **_Temperance_**
14 **_The Fool_**
Who do I think I am?

21 **_Six of Cups_**
22 **_Seven of Cups_**
What else is new?

9 **_Three of Wands_**
10 **_The Hierophant_**
What's in store for me?

11 **_Ten of Swords_**
12 **_Temperance_**
What are my options?
Where am I?

1 **_Ace of Wands_**
2 **_Knight of Cups_**

3 **_King of Swords_**
4 **_The Magician_**
What's in my way?

7 **_Five of Wands_**
8 **_Five of Wands_**
What's been happening?

5 **_Nine of Pentacles_**
6 **_Four of Swords_**
Where have I been?

⟨TAROTSCAPE⟩

As the two cards for each heartprint are named, lay them out for your own observation. On Worksheet #1, fill in the cards drawn and their meanings. Take plenty of time to look up meanings (Chapters 3 and 4) and symbology (Chapter 8) if you need to.

Also, for maximum learning, write your stance and heartlink statements before comparing your answers with those made by the reader and before drawing the next pair of cards.

We have added a commentary after each heartprint which was taken from the reader's interaction with the querents.

After you have compared your responses on Worksheet #1 with those in this chapter, complete Worksheets #2 and #3.

Again, compare your responses with those on the completed worksheets at the end of the chapter. How do your perspectives compare with those of the actual reader? What were you more sensitive to? What do you think the reader missed? How does your approach differ?

Congratulate yourself on taking another major step toward developing your own Tarot for Two reading style.

If you are going to work along with the reader (Exercise 15), here is your situation as it was presented to the Tarot reader. A couple come to you for a reading with the question "What is the matter with our communication?" The husband asks the wife which deck she wants to represent her, and after a silent deliberation, she selects the smaller deck.

Now, turn the page to see the first two cards drawn and begin filling in Worksheet #1, The Heartbeat of the Relationship, for this couple.

Worksheet #1

The Heartbeat of the Relationship

Person 1   Husband

Person 2   Wife

Question   What is the matter with our
            communication?

WHERE AM I?

Cards: P1 Ace of Wands   P2 Knight of Cups

Meanings	*Stances*	*Heartlink*
1. New beginning.	He is ready for a new beginning.	Both want to resolve the issue, but with different approaches.
2. Emotionally intense; practical plans.	She has an emotional investment and wants to work it out in a practical way.	

Commentary:

He looks for more growth in the relationship through better communication. He realizes something new is needed and wants to take the lead in developing it for the two of them. The light gray indicates his willingness to compromise.

She brings emotional intensity to the situation, but she also looks on this opportunity as a practical way to improve the situation, an opportunity to work out better understandings. She wants to change, and sees this as an opportunity to express love.

WHAT'S IN MY WAY ?

Cards: P1 King of Swords   P2 The Magician
                                          (Major Arcana I)

Worksheet #1 (cont.)

Meanings	*Stances*	*Heartlink*
3. Able; assertive.	He needs to be assertive.	They need to modify their individual approaches.
4. Confidence; skill through practice.	She needs to be confident and develop her relationship skills.	

Commentary:

His problem is to be more assertive or open about his position and feelings, yet be sensitive to her communication. He needs to maintain his own integrity and self-expression without becoming bossy.

Her problem lies in not using her mental abilities and practical know-how to make decisions as well as he does. She wants to fuse inner spiritual or intuitive "knowing" with practicality. Her challenge is to bring more depth, options, and a sense of permanence (eternity symbol) into their communication. She may try to make too big a deal of every issue.

Micro-Cross Statement

The absence of Pentacles suggests there has been a lot of thinking and emoting about this issue but very little work. He comes into the situation more intuitive about the issue than she and can help her rely on her own intuition more, but he needs to achieve a mental balance (14 and 4 + 1 = 5) for himself by becoming more active in his communication. For their mutual success, she needs to become more active in making choices (1) and in decisions about her own personal development aside from the relationship.

Worksheet #1 (cont.)

WHERE HAVE I BEEN?

Cards: P1 Nine of Pentacles   P2 Four of Swords

Meanings	Stances	Heartlink
5. Independent; abundant accomplishments.	He's used to success from his efforts.	They have been meeting their separate needs rather than
6. Redefining needs; introspection.	She has reevaluated and redefined her needs.	working toward joint goals as a couple.

Commentary:
  He has functioned successfully and felt things went well. He attained financial stability and prosperity and enjoyed the process.
  She has let her own assertiveness rest and has turned within, using meditation, possibly, and introspection. She directed her attention toward her own spiritual needs and growth.

WHAT'S BEEN HAPPENING?

Cards: P1 Five of Wands   P2 Five of Wands

Meanings	Stances	Heartlink
7. Competitive; struggle; balancing.	Both have gained an awareness of the need to balance each other.	Both bring skills of being able to balance things out, but the competitiveness of one or both of them contributes to the problem.
8. (Same as above.)		

Worksheet #1 (cont.)

Commentary:
Recently, he has reordered his priorities, feeling that he can improve communication with his wife, intuitively knowing that he can establish something better between them. This card and the Where am I? card show a good grasp of the situation and a willingness to grow (buds on the Wands).

The card duplication indicates they are, indeed, in tune with each other. She has recently been aware of the need for reevaluation and for growth. These duplicate cards make it apparent why they are able to be here together in the spirit of cooperation and a shared venture—each struggling within for ideas to establish priorities beneficial to their relationship. Also, both have recognized an element of competition in the relationship.

Person 1   Husband _____

_____

_____

WHAT'S IN STORE FOR ME?

		The Hierophant
Cards:	P1 Three of Wands	P2 (Major Arcana X)

	Meanings	*Stances*	*Heartlink*
9.	Commitment; energetic.	He will be more enthusiastic about their relationship.	New modes of interacting: she teaches; he cooperates.
10.	Hearing the inner teacher.	She will be open to her intuition.	

Commentary:
He will be able to make new adjustments, realizing that his rewards will come. He will find that cooperation is right for him at this time of his life, that it "makes sense" (the yellow in the card), and he will feel like committing to more interaction.

Worksheet #1 (cont.)

If she will listen to her inner voice, she can teach him. She can assume this role with him as she has in the past within herself (Four of Swords for Where have I been?). She can help the new interaction by setting conventional rules, tried and tested ways from their past.

WHAT ARE MY OPTIONS ?

Cards: P1 <u>Ten of Swords</u> P2 <u>Temperance (Major Arcana XIV)</u>

	Meanings	*Stances*	*Heartlink*
11.	Transformed viewpoints; end of strife.	He can see changes are necessary.	They can try new methods.
12.	Harmony; understanding.	She can understand and encourage him.	

<u>Commentary:</u>

If he lets the past, purely rational approach go, it will release them from the limitations of communication they have been experiencing. He will understand how he has been burdened and can be open to a new approach. He will be ready for a new level of closeness (no Cups in the spread yet).

She can have a feeling of release as she experiences a new level of interaction. She will be able to blend their temperaments as he puts to rest some of his bluster and she becomes more aware of the inner strength she can bring to the relationship.

WHO DO I THINK I AM ?

Cards: P1 <u>Temperance (Major Arcana XIV)</u> P2 <u>The Fool (Major Arcana 0)</u>

	Meanings	*Stances*	*Heartlink*
13.	Understanding; interaction.	He considers himself the more understanding-	Neither is taking responsibility for clear communication.

Worksheet #1 (cont.)

	Meanings	**Stances**	**Heartlink**
14.	Adventurous;	one in	
	unaware.	the relationship.	
		She is unaware of her	
		role in the problem.	

Commentary:

He perceives himself as a man of compromise and negotiation, able to see both sides of an issue and then act on principle—a person of modification, able to blend and understand. Perhaps he has suppressed it in his business striving, and developed a habit of denying this aspect of himself. But this part of his character will enable him to make necessary adjustments.

Her fearless nature in approaching life's journey gives her courage in their relationship to go ahead with confidence about what she can bring to it. She sees herself as ever-youthful in spirit and welcomes this chance to improve their communication.

WHAT'S OUT THERE FOR ME?

			Judgement
Cards:	P1 Seven of Swords		P2 (Major Arcana XX)

	Meanings	**Stances**	**Heartlink**
15.	Independent action;	His manipulative	Their discrimination
	manipulation.	communication is	will be sharpened.
16.	Release from illusion.	exposed. She sees his	
		behavior in a new light.	

Commentary:

He will plan and carry out new ways of communicating and seeing results—making points and comparisons. He will apply his business talents to the relationship in a constructive manner.

She will evaluate the relationship and accept a more realistic approach in dealing with him on mundane issues. She will experience a new level of awareness and consciousness and, by her example, show a developing spirituality (the blue in the card).

Worksheet #1 (cont.)

WHAT DO I EXPECT?

Cards: P1 The Devil (Major Arcana XV) _____   P2 Knight of Pentacles _____

Meanings	*Stances*	*Heartlink*
17. Misunderstanding. _____ _____ _____ _____ _____	He is afraid that if he adopts a new way of communicating, he will be at a disadvantage.	Although both are afraid of losing something, they both nevertheless expect to compensate for their one-sided approach to
18. Stability; hard worker. _____ _____ _____ _____	She is afraid she will have to assume most of the responsibility for a change in their communication.	the issue. _____ _____ _____

Commentary:

He hopes to be free of the limitations that he imposed on himself through years of suppressing the inner side of his nature (keeping to himself in the garden—Nine of Pentacles for Where have I been?). He wishes to slip from the chains of materialistic thinking and be open to insights and feelings that she can share with him.

She hopes to incorporate a more methodical, deliberate way into her approach to their communication. She wants to become more grounded and practical without damage to her self-esteem.

WHERE DOES ALL THIS LEAD ?

Cards: P1 Queen of Swords _____   P2 The Sun (Major Arcana XIX) _____

Worksheet #1 (cont.)

	Meanings	**Stances**	**Heartlink**
19.	Compassion; wisdom-tempered logic.	He uses his feminine side to temper his approach.	They switch approaches to create a better stage for communication.
20.	Creativity; leadership.	She draws upon her masculine aspects for a new approach.	

Commentary:

His communication will be increased by his developing spirituality (blue) and the use of logic, tempered with compassion and a sense of fairness. As he becomes more aware of the feminine qualities within himself that give him strength, he will be able to recognize her ability to make decisions and will respect her more as a partner.

She will use her creativity in new ways of communicating joy and play to him. Feeling more comfortable with the masculine strength in herself, she will take the lead at times.

WHAT ELSE IS NEW?

Cards: P1 Six of Cups   P2 Seven of Cups

	Meanings	**Stances**	**Heartlink**
21.	Concern for family; harmony.	His love will give him the courage to communicate more openly.	Emotional bonds will sustain them during their efforts to practice new skills and ways of being.
22.	Imagination; abundant choices.	She has many new choices in how to communicate with him.	

Worksheet #1 (cont.)

Commentary:

He will be enriched by letting go of some of the rigid patterns of the past and letting his childlike side come back into his life. This should bring him to a better balance with her and in his dealings with other people as well. Their love for one another will help maintain harmony.

She will experience an abundance of ideas and fantasies to draw upon in focusing and directing her energies. However, she needs to avoid following all the plans and desires which occur to her and concentrate on those on which they both agree.

Insights

He: I now realize I can tell her—and she wants to hear—some of my thinking that I've kept to myself. She: It's a relief to know we both are willing to work on our personal issues to resolve our question. _____
_____
_____
_____

Plan(s) of Action

She: I will return to doing some active things I like to fulfill me rather than expecting to get it all from our relationship, and I will become more active in planning things we can do together. He: I will remind myself she is not other people from my past even when what she does reminds me of them. And I will tell her about it when it happens so when can talk about it.

Worksheet #2

Heartstyles

Person 1 <u>Husband</u>   Person 2 <u>Wife</u>

Question <u>What is the matter with our communication?</u> Date <u>_____</u>

Where am I?	Both want to resolve the issue, but with different approaches.	They can see the necessity for modifying their approaches and
Where have I been?	They have been meeting their separate needs rather than working toward joint goals as a couple.	establishing joint goals.

Current or long-standing viewpoints

*   *

Where have I been?	They have been meeting their separate needs rather than working toward joint goals as a couple.	They have the skill to work together toward a single goal. Competitiveness separates their team focus.
What's been happening?	Both bring skills of being able to "balance things out," but the competitiveness of one or both of them contributes to the problem.	

Possible changes
affecting
the interaction

Worksheet #2 (cont.)

Heartprints	**Heartlinks**	**Heartstyle**
What's in my way?	They need to modify their individual approaches.	Their new approach needs to include changing roles; she leads; he cooperates.
What's in store for me?	New modes of interacting: she teaches; he cooperates.	
		Effects of acceptance or rejection of challenge
	*	*
Where am I?	Both want to resolve the issue, but with different approaches.	Clear communication requires clarifying goals in joint terms.
Who do I think I am?	Neither is taking responsibility for clear communication.	
		How outer behavior conforms to inner belief
	*	*
What are my options?	They can try new methods.	In spite of their fears, they work together.
What do I expect?	Although both are afraid of losing something, they both nevertheless expect to compensate for their one-sided approach to the issue.	
		Are expectations realistic for unfolding potential?

Worksheet #3

Power Patterns

Person 1 ___Husband___   Person 2 ___Wife___

Question ___What is the matter with our communication?___   Date ___

		Tally	Pattern Interpretation
1. Major Arcana	P-1	2	He does not have as much inner investment in the question and is willing to take action.
	P-2	6	She has a great potential, and resources, for inner growth.
2. Court Cards	P-1	2	[King; Queen] He assumes the authority.
	P-2	2	[Knight; Knight] She is the doer. They are concerned with themselves rather than with outsiders.
3. Suits			
Wands	P-1	3	He operates intuitively and can grow through new experience.
	P-2	1	
Cups	P-1	1	
	P-2	2	
Swords	P-1	4	He brings a competitive attitude
	P-2	1	tempered with discrimination.

Worksheet #3 (cont.)

		Tally	**Pattern Interpretation**
Pentacles	P-1	1	_____
	P-2	1	_____
4. Duplicate	P-1	3-5s	Both are at a point of choice.
Numbers	P-2	3-5s	They can now decide the
			direction they choose to go in.
5. Duplicate	P-1	2	Five of Wands in the same heartprint shows
Cards	P-2	2	that both need to deal with issues of
			competition and communication.
			Temperance in different heartprints shows
			their ability to express understanding.

Chapter 15

What Do My Garden and I Need from One Another?
(A Tarotscape for a Project)

From time to time many of us talk to our favorite inanimate objects, as well as to those that frustrate us. When was the last time you were in a hurry and silently, or otherwise, cursed a stalled car in front of you or a bank computer that was down?

For a number of years now, it has been fashionable to talk to plants. The movie *On a Clear Day You Can See Forever* featured a woman who talked to her plants. (She also heard them talk back; most of us don't.)

The people of the Findhorn Community in England grow plants and vegetables where it was once said that nothing but sand and weeds could exist. In part they attribute their success to regular consultation with devas (energy forces that govern the plant kingdom) about what the plants like and dislike.

The woman who requested this reading spoke to her flowers and respected the spirit of her garden, which she was in the process of re-designing. Her question was, "What do my garden and I need from one another?"

She liked the idea of using different decks, and the reader offered her a choice from the decks with which he was comfortable reading.

Since she had dialogued with her garden extensively in her journal and thought it had a sense of humor, she chose the "Du Wacky Du" (Morgan's Tarot) deck for the garden and the Rider-Waite deck for herself. She decided the garden's deck would be on the bottom, the first card drawn for each heartprint.

This chapter begins with a completed Tarot for Two Tarotscape Record to show the entire layout. Two completed worksheets follow. A Power Patterns worksheet is not included, because using the worksheet requires two Rider-Waite, or comparable, decks which employ the same tallying categories. Morgan's Tarot is not a standard deck, nor does it have categories comparable to Rider-Waite categories. All cards are of equal value and are unnumbered.

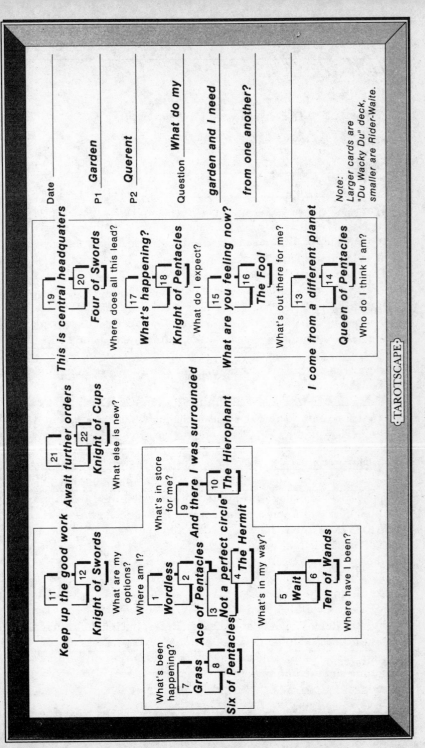

Date _____

P1 Garden

P2 Querent

Question What do my

garden and I need

from one another?

This is central headquaters

19 | 20
Four of Swords
Where does all this lead?

17 | 18
What's happening?
Knight of Pentacles
What do I expect?

15 | 16
What are you feeling now?
The Fool
What's out there for me?

13 | 14
I come from a different planet
Queen of Pentacles
Who do I think I am?

Note:
Larger cards are
"Du Wacky Du" deck,
smaller are Rider-Waite.

Keep up the good work Await further orders

21 | 22
Knight of Cups
What else is new?

11 | 12
Knight of Swords
What are my options?
Where am I?

9
What's in store for me?

And there I was surrounded
10
The Hierophant

1 | 2
Wordless
Ace of Pentacles

Not a perfect circle
3 | 4
The Hermit
What's in my way?

7 | 8
What's been happening?
Grass Ace of Pentacles
Six of Pentacles

5 | 6
Wait
Ten of Wands
Where have I been?

‹TAROTSCAPE›

Worksheet #1

The Heartbeat of the Relationship

Person 1   The Garden

Person 2   Querent

Date

Question   What do my garden and I need from

one another?

WHERE AM I?

Cards: P1 Wordless   P2 Ace of Pentacles

Meanings	*Stances*	*Heartlink*
1. Nonverbal messages are being sent.	The garden does communicate with her.	She needs to look at the garden, be sensitive to its
2. Initiative; power to do.	Take action.	messages, and take action.

WHAT'S IN MY WAY?

Cards: P1 Not a perfect circle   P2 The Hermit (Major Arcana IX)

Meanings	*Stances*	*Heartlink*
3. It is a perfect whatever-it-is.	To make it the best it can be.	The garden is waiting for your activity.
4. Wisdom of experience; healer.	Use your own ideas and methods.	

Worksheet #1 (cont.)

Micro-Cross Statement

She sees the garden's signals and comes into the situation actively expressing her own need and ability to take positive action. The garden will respond in its natural way if she uses her own intuition to heal or attend to it. If she gets busy and puts her ideas into action, both she and the garden will be successful (9 symbology).

WHERE HAVE I BEEN?

Cards: P1 Wait   P2 Ten of Wands

Meanings	*Stances*	*Heartlink*
5. A certain gestation period is required.	It had to grow into what you see.	It reverted to its nature and wants you
6. Foundation for next cycle.	Its natural growth is your challenge.	to organize it.

WHAT'S BEEN HAPPENING?

Cards: P1 Grass   P2 Six of Pentacles

Meanings	*Stances*	*Heartlink*
7. Overgrown.	It has grown to get your attention.	The garden wants weeding and feeding.
8. Willingness to share.	You want to help it grow beautifully.	

Worksheet #1 (cont.)

WHAT'S IN STORE FOR ME?

Cards: P1 And there I was surrounded _____ P2 The Hierophant (Major Arcana V) _____

Meanings	*Stances*	*Heartlink*
9. You and the earth are one.	The garden wants to express you.	You need to be more sensitive to the
10. Inner hearing; inner teacher.	You want to know what will make the garden happy.	garden's needs, which, after all, are not so different from your own.

WHAT ARE MY OPTIONS?

Cards: P1 Keep up the good work _____ P2 Knight of Swords _____

Meanings	*Stances*	*Heartlink*
11. A sense of purpose can produce surprising results.	It wants you to plan its growth.	The garden will be happy with what you do.
12. Skill; champion.	You have the skill to do it.	

WHO DO I THINK I AM?

Cards: P1 I come from a different planet. _____ P2 Queen of Pentacles _____

Meanings	*Stances*	*Heartlink*
13. Feeling of alienation.	It feels you don't understand it.	You need to communicate with it

Worksheet #1 (cont.)

	Meanings	**Stances**	**Heartlink**
14.	Fruitful efforts; generous.	You can give to it.	more.

WHAT'S OUT THERE FOR ME?

Cards: P1 <u>What are you feeling now?</u> P2 <u>The Fool (Major Arcana 0)</u>

	Meanings	**Stances**	**Heartlink**
15.	Awareness of the present moment.	Good time to plant.	The time and place is right now.
16.	Adventure; choice without fear.	Just start anywhere.	

WHAT DO I EXPECT?

Cards: P1 <u>What's happening?</u> P2 <u>Knight of Pentacles</u>

	Meanings	**Stances**	**Heartlink**
17.	An innocent question.	Garden doesn't know what to expect.	The garden wants you to work in it, and it
18.	Overseer; hard worker.	It needs a lot of work.	will be happy.

WHERE DOES ALL THIS LEAD?

Cards: P1 <u>This is central headquarters.</u> P2 <u>Four of Swords</u>

Worksheet #1 (cont.)

	Meanings	Stances	Heartlink
19.	The heart chakra or the sun.	Cleaning needs to be done so the sun can get to the plants.	Use your heart and intuition to create a beautiful garden.
20.	Turning inward.	Use your intuition.	

WHAT ELSE IS NEW?

Cards:　P1 Await further orders.　　　P2 Knight of Cups

	Meanings	Stances	Heartlink
21.	More data is coming.	The garden will communicate.	As you work with the garden, you will be inspired.
22.	New beginnings; change of direction.	You will see different things to do.	

Insights

Well, I knew my garden and I were friends and good for each other, and this reading just confirmed it. My garden is probably more forgiving than I would be.

Plan(s) of Action

I'd better get home and get to work, but I think I need to tune in to the nature of my garden more, rather than just going along with what I think.

Worksheet #2

Heartstyles

Person 1 ___Garden___   Person 2 ___Querent___

Question ___What do my garden and I need from___   Date _____

___one another?___

Heartprints	*Heartlinks*	*Heartstyle*
Where am I?	She needs to look at the garden, be sensitive to its messages, and take action.	It wants your guidance.
Where have I been?	It reverted to its nature and wants you to organize it.	
		Current or long-standing viewpoints
	*	*
Where have I been?	It reverted to its nature and wants you to organize it.	It needs your help.
What's been happening?	The garden wants weeding and feeding.	
		Possible changes affecting the interaction
	*	*
What's in my way?	The garden is waiting for your activity. You need to be more	It wants and needs your feeding it, nurturing and organizing it.

Worksheet #2 (cont.)

Heartprints	**Heartlinks**	**Heartstyle**
What's in store for me?	sensitive to the garden's needs, which, after all, are not so different from your own.	
		Effects of acceptance or rejection of challenges
	*	*
Where am I?	The garden needs weeding, and care.	You need to become physically involved with it.
Who do I think I am?	You need to communicate with it more.	
		How outer behavior conforms to inner belief
	*	*
What are my options?	The garden will be happy with your efforts.	All it takes is a little work for
What do I expect?	The garden wants you to work in it, and it will be happy.	your garden to be happy.
		Are expectations realistic for unfolding potential?
	*	*

Chapter 16

What Are the Advantages and Obstacles of Nan's Writing a Mystery with Betty? (Two Women Consider Collaborating)

In the 1940s the radio announcer for the soap opera "The Romance of Helen Trent" used to open the program by asking, "Can a woman from a small mining town in the West find success and happiness in the big city?"

Taking our cue from him, we might likewise ask, "Can two women from a large Southern California city find success and happiness writing a mystery together? Will their different lifestyles and motivations lead them to confine murder and mayhem to their book, or cause them to bring it into their collaborative relationship?"

Stay tuned for an episode of "whodunit" from the annals of the Tarot for Two.

Nan and Betty (not their real names) came to us for insight on the possibility of their writing a mystery, which they had been discussing for about a month. They had never collaborated before. Due to a family emergency, only one of the querents, Nan, was able to be present. So the agreed-upon question became, "What are the advantages and obstacles of Nan's writing a mystery with Betty?"

This chapter demonstrates a Tarot for Two interpretation which has been condensed and edited from the actual transcript of the reading. It shows the impressions that result when two readers build on one another's ideas, sharing their understandings, even when they interpret some of the cards' elements differently. (Conversation between the querent and the readers has been eliminated for brevity; therefore, some of the original interactional flow has been sacrificed.)

Robert represented Betty, the absent querent. Signe read for Nan, who selected and shuffled the larger deck for herself. Robert shuffled the smaller deck for Betty.

WHERE AM I?

Nan's card: Two of Pentacles
   Signe: Nan is able to handle her part and work with another.
Betty's card: Four of Wands
   Robert: Betty brings liveliness to the project. The yellow sky and ground show she has the mental ability to do the work.
   Signe: Betty looks at the project as having fun with Nan. Therefore, you two start out with slightly different motivations.

WHAT'S IN MY WAY?

Nan's card: Queen of Swords
   Signe: Nan has the authority to make the decisions. Since this is the challenge heartprint, her action in the relationship may be that of taking charge and making the decisions, perhaps enforcing or getting Betty to act upon her decisions.
   Robert: Nan has the ability to stay on top of the project, to take control.
   Signe: The frivolity Betty brings to the project may be thwarted by Nan's practicality.
   Robert: Having to get things done, meet deadlines, may change Betty's energies and the lightness she brings to the project.
   Signe: This card can involve contracts, and Nan and Betty may need to consider creating a formal agreement between them.
Betty's card: The Hanged Man (Major Arcana XII)
   Robert: Betty sees things completely upside down from the way they are, or from Nan's position as the Queen of Swords.
   Signe: Betty's challenge could be to change her mind and be flexible enough to go along with Nan's structure.
   Robert: Being the Queen of Swords, Nan is very stable. She has the ability; the clouds show mental activity. Nan has her feet on the ground, but Betty's feet are in the air. If they work together, Betty may have to do a turnaround, or stand on her own feet.
   Signe: Betty's problem is her inability to look at things in a different way. She has to be able to change her mind, change her approach.
   Robert: Betty's approach works for her, but it may not work when you two are collaborating.

WHERE HAVE I BEEN?

Nan's card: The Devil (Major Arcana XV)

Signe: These are underlying factors and past occurrences that bring Nan to this point in time. It is also seeing the illusion of the world. Because of previous experience, Nan sees through the appearances and perceives that this collaboration may cause her problems.

Robert: The way out of illusion is laughing at it. The chains in the card are real, although removable. Both Nan and Betty need to examine what they've done in the past with other people. Where, in working with other people, did they fall down with respect to their own illusions?

Signe: Nan realizes she has found herself trapped in the past and wonders how much this and the illusion of working smoothly together will affect the future. Will past patterns surface and continue?

Betty's card: also The Devil (Major Arcana XV)

Robert: And this is Betty's same problem, dealing with her illusions.

Signe: Her past also fits her patterns. We haven't used the word "manipulation," but I think it fits here. You both have been manipulated and been the manipulators.

Robert: Nan needs to look at her illusions, and—especially with the Queen of Swords—at how the work and the finances are going to be divided.

Signe: And their illusions about the glamour of the project, the glamour they may be putting on it.

WHAT'S BEEN HAPPENING?

Nan's card: Nine of Wands

Signe: About a week or ten days ago Nan began having intuitive, second thoughts—Wands are intuition. In the past she has apparently done well in writing with other people and knows intuitively that she can collaborate. Because it's almost, but not quite, the completion of this cycle—nine, not yet 10—there's still something within herself she needs to deal with.

Robert: The Nine of Wands is a triple completion. Nan may have done this before. She needs to look at those three other times. She has plenty of ideas (Wands) behind her, but she's wary about the present idea.

Signe: I interpret the Wands in the background as an accumulation of things Nan has done. Right now, in having second thoughts, she is looking back at those.

Betty's card: *Nine of Swords*

Robert: Betty is not really paying attention to her abilities. And the nine, again, is a triple completion—things she already has completed. But the cover of the bed, which she's not looking at, has all the power: the roses of passion, the yellow of the mental, plus all the astrological and mathematical symbols. All the power is there. She needs to open her eyes and see that she has the power to do this collaboration, using the talents she already has developed.

Signe: I interpret this as Betty wanting to let go of writing practical things and get into writing for fun and fantasy. She thinks she can be freer in this kind of writing.

WHAT'S IN STORE FOR ME?

Nan's card: *Judgement (Major Arcana XX)*

Signe: In a few days, a week or so, material may emerge from the unconscious—new insights, hearing the inner voice. A dream or an actual experience could trigger a different understanding of what is involved and how Nan should handle it.

Robert: I connect this card with The Devil card, and with both Nan's and Betty's illusions. The raised arms of the three people in the foremost coffins symbolize the letters LVX, which means light, seeing the light, being the light. In this case, it would mean seeing the ideas from the recent past, or what to do, and then seeing the illusions that Nan has been working under.

Signe: I also see this as a card of hearing, so something will strike Nan and she'll really hear it.

Robert: Or when Nan is talking with Betty about this, she'll hear the interaction differently. Both Nan and Betty have to sit down and confront their illusions.

Betty's card: *Two of Pentacles*

Robert: This is the card Nan started with. Balancing out material things. Betty is going to have to start in the next seven to ten days to decide how to balance this collaboration into her life; how to work it in with the rest of her obligations.

WHAT ARE MY OPTIONS?

Nan's card: King of Swords

Signe: Nan's challenge here is to assume the authority; to have her feminine aspect make the decision to be the authoritative one. She's already quite able to assume that authority in a masculine, take-charge way. That's the King.

Robert: Nan's choice on the mundane level—about the job, about the writing—is that of being the one to make the decisions. The sword is the decision. Two-edged, it cuts both ways. If Nan learns whatever lessons are here, she'll have the ability—the power within her—to be the King of Swords, whether she takes the stance or not.

Betty's card: Two of Swords

Robert: Now Betty is at the other end in balancing two abilities. Her eyes are covered, including her third eye. Both her intuition and her physical sight are blinded. She's balanced, ready to go one way or the other. There may be another project that Betty feels she has to do at the same time that Nan and Betty are working. And with her Two of Pentacles in the What's in store for me? heartprint, she will have to balance and dance between the two. [Nan confirms that Betty has another writing project that excites her.] Betty may have to consider, in dealing with her illusions, whether she can balance the two, can turn her world upside down to meet the schedules for the collaboration and for her project. And then the Nine of Swords in the What's been happening? heartprint raises the question of which to do, which of her abilities to use. She's got the abilities. She's got the happiness and the joy with the Four of Wands in the Where am I? heartprint. She's got the illusions. She's got the talents also. So it can work out, but it's going to be work for her.

Signe: Betty needs to be able to turn her mind around and see and accept another viewpoint. She's going to be forced to look at the two mental aspects of what's going on with herself.

WHO DO I THINK I AM?

Nan's card: Ten of Cups

Signe: The Ten of Cups is completion, and a very happy emotional outlook. Nan sees this collaboration as expressing the very best of her thoughts about how people act in life, as an expression of happiness and fulfillment. Even though the project is a mystery, she

intends to show the characters as full people. The basis of her writing—her purpose and intent—is to write it from an aspect of fulfillment, rather than trying to prove something to the world. She is
writing it as a flowering of herself. [Nan confirms this perception.]
Robert: Cups are, for me, plans. The Ten of Cups here says that to
work with people and with someone is the most fun you can have.
It's going to be work, but it's like family. When you work with people, you really get to know them. And both of your inner children
come out to play. The rainbow promises there's going to be a completion of some sort.
Signe: And the characters in the book, too. They're going to be full
and expressive.

Betty's card: King of Cups
Robert: We've got the Ten of Cups to the King of Cups. These are
the plans. Betty sees herself in the collaboration as having a very
forceful or powerful plan. Or, she feels she has good insight into
the power of the book.
Signe: Betty feels from her experiences in life that she really knows
about the dynamics, how people interact emotionally.

WHAT'S OUT THERE FOR ME?

Nan's card: Death (Major Arcana XIII)
Signe: This is the energy that will be going along with you during
the planning and perhaps as you're working together: transformation, changing your thoughts to produce something new. Throughout this project you'll be letting go of unnecessary things you realize
you no longer need for this particular project . . . letting go and
making room for new, fresh, humorous things. I see humor coming
into this all along. [Nan confirms that Betty wants to write a humorous mystery.] I never read this card as humor entering, but I
see it with this spread. Letting go of what you might have held onto
in thinking about what's proper for a mystery and putting in your
own innovations.
Robert: The Death card with The Devil relates to letting go of illusions you've had about writing or working with people in the past
and illusions about how much to give in and change your ideas—
how flexible you were in the past and how much, or how little, it
got you. So, with The Devil in the Where have I been? heartprint,
and with Death as a transition, what your proposed collaboration
has to offer is the death of some of those illusions.

Betty's card: The Moon (Major Arcana XVIII)

Robert: The environment offers a different path for Betty. The Moon is insight, reflection. For her, this may be reflecting on the past—back to The Devil and her illusions. It's the sun eclipsed, a lunar eclipse. So we're talking about her male power being overshadowed by her female side. This writing may give her the chance of allowing her feminine, receptive side to be more active.

Signe: The Moon, of course, represents the unconscious. Betty could get some strong insights from material surfacing from the wellspring of her own unconscious.

Robert: Because her previous card is the King of Cups, her male side has been in charge. Now The Moon is eclipsing the male side so that her feminine side can emerge.

WHAT DO I EXPECT?

Nan's card: Eight of Pentacles

Signe: This is a card of work, of piling up an accumulation of accomplishment, but also of learning new skills.

Robert: I'd say the Eight of Pentacles is structure. He creates each pentacle, drawing the five points, connecting the lines. Each chapter has to be created.

Signe: And, of course, they represent money, too. You want to make money.

Robert: Money, money, money. Work, work, work.

Betty's card: Six of Pentacles

Robert: Betty wants to come from a place of balance, but she may give more to one project than to the other.

Signe: She wants to be more fair on this project with Nan than she's perhaps been in some of her other dealings in life. She wants this as a balancing factor at this point in her life.

WHERE DOES ALL THIS LEAD?

Nan's card: Nine of Swords

Signe: This relates to the outcome. It represents letting go of mental restrictions. For this project, Nan will let go of some of the rules she has adhered to, perhaps in her writing, perhaps in her own mental outlook.

Robert: Nan's not seeing her power. The two cards she also has to consider are the King of Swords and the triple completion of the

Nine of Swords. Nan's going to use her abilities as she hasn't used them before, and she's going to change. It will be like waking from a deep sleep.

Signe: Swords are discrimination, getting to the real heart of something. Nan will come to a point of cutting through the morass of the unnecessary and sticking to what is just right for this particular story.

Betty's card: Five of Wands

Robert: This is a sharing of ideas, sharing Betty's intuition. The way the Wands are being handled, they almost make a pentacle, and that means manifestation of her ideas.

Signe: Because the five is the practical level of man more than the seven, Betty's intuitive faculties will be working on a very practical level in this project.

WHAT ELSE IS NEW?

Nan's card: The Hierophant (Major Arcana V)

Signe: Okay, this is a summary card. It is the card of the inner teacher, another card of hearing. The Judgement card is of hearing, and so is the Hierophant. This heartprint supplements those adjacent to it: What are my options? and Where does all this lead?. Nan will have the guidance of her inner teacher as she uses her decision-making and newly developing skills. Again, I get the comedy aspects. She will have some guidance as to how to proceed as she opens up to those aspects.

Robert: I see the inner guide as what you need to start with to define and eliminate your illusions. The Eight of Pentacles [What do I expect?] is the mundane work of doing the writing. The Swords represents bringing your talents together, but also having to work at it. And then changing from the feminine—gentle, receptive—to the King of Swords, the masculine, doing.

Betty's card: Two of Wands

Robert: Again, ideas or intuition. We're back to another two, which is a dichotomy of the world of ideas. We have the ideas—Wands—the Swords, which is the abilities, and then we have the Pentacles, which is manifestation. Betty's going to really have to make a choice about what to manifest.

Signe: Betty's going to have to face these two aspects of things as she goes along, whether she intends to or not. She has three twos, every one except the Two of Cups. She ends up understanding much more about her own inner dichotomies.

Robert: And also her illusions. The Hanged Man turning her world upside down means Betty seeing her illusions. Balancing with the Two of Pentacles [What's in store for me?] means seeing what she's going to do, making a decision. The Two of Swords [What are my options?] asks, "How am I going to cut this and cut that at the same time? Can I cut it?" And then, the outcome of her internal interaction is two new ideas. Because Nan's inner teacher [The Hierophant] is beneath the Two of Wands, she'll be helping Betty if she wants it.

Signe: The Two of Wands gives a broad outlook. As she's gaining more insight into herself from this subconscious area of The Moon card [What's out there for me?], she will have a more comfortable outlook on the world in general.

Robert: The thing to focus on is the Where have I been? cards. Both Nan and Betty have The Devil. It may look like the same illusion because the cards are the same, but all illusions are different. Working together, getting the book written, is going to eliminate these illusions or bring them up for you to do something with. That's the true work.

Signe: The two cards of the past [Where have I been? and What's been happening?] are very important: the Queen of Swords and The Hanged Man. Because of her illusions, Nan's challenge will be to make certain decisions and stick with them—to discriminate, to get a certain mind-set and use it. And Betty is challenged to expand her perspective and to see two points of view.

Robert: For Betty, we start off with a happy time and that's her way. It does change the energy. And she has had to look at it upside down, as The Hanged Man. Now it's time to turn around. She has to turn right side up and see the illusions that have been created from having to make fun of everything as a defense.

Signe: You both certainly will have a very interesting learning time with these two cards—Death and The Moon—because one is transformation, rebirth, coming out, and the other is probing the depths underneath. But, of course, they're both learning and, in a sense, bring transformation.

{TAROTSCAPE}

Date _____

P1 _Nan_

P2 _Betty_

Question _What are the_

advantages and

obstacles of Nan's

writing a mystery with

Betty?

The Hierophant

└ 21
└ 22 **Two of Wands**

What else is new?

King of Swords

└ 11
└ 12 **Two of Swords**

What are my options?

Where am I?

Two of Pentacles

└ 1
└ 2 **Four of Wands**

What's in store for me?

└ 9 **Judgement**
└ 10 **Two of Pentacles**

Queen of Swords

└ 3
└ 4 **The Hanged Man**

What's in my way?

Nine of Wands

└ 7
└ 8 **Nine of Swords**

What's been happening?

The Devil

└ 5
└ 6 **The Devil**

Where have I been?

Nine of Swords

└ 19
└ 20 **Five of Wands**

Where does all this lead?

Eight of Pentacles

└ 17
└ 18 **Six of Pentacles**

What do I expect?

└ 15 **Death**
└ 16 **The Moon**

What's out there for me?

Ten of Cups

└ 13
└ 14 **King of Cups**

Who do I think I am?

Part 6

Heartscapes

Tarot Tutor 6

Time is
Too Slow for those who Wait,
Too Swift for those who Fear,
Too Long for those who Grieve,
Too Short for those who Rejoice,
But for those who Love
Time is not.[87]

Although the poet reminds us that time is relative, we'd be the first to tell you that Tarot for Two takes time. There are days—and times—when you just don't want to do a complete Tarot for Two. Or, you've already done one for a particular relationship and would like to take just a tiny little peek into what's in store for you today without having to create another full Tarotscape. We know. We know.

That's why we created the four new accessory layouts presented in Chapter 17. They help you keep abreast of your relationship progress in between Tarot for Two readings. Several of them give you additional information not provided by your original Tarotscape.

And for those special times when you'd like to relish a Tarot reading, make it something momentous, Chapter 18 teaches a growth ritual which you and another can enact.

The ceremony, performed when you want to bask in celebratory time, results in the creation of a guiding Tarot mandala for the next year or next major phase in your relationship.

---

[87]For Katrina's Sun-Dial. *The Poems of Henry Van Dyke*, 1920, p. 259.

Performed annually, the mandala growth ritual is an excellent way to honor completions and new beginnings in an ongoing relationship. It is particularly appropriate when any of the following cards appear in the Where does all this lead? or What else is new? heartprint: Wheel of Fortune, Death, Four of Wands, Three of Cups, and the nines of any suit.

So whether your plans are to rush through the day or to slowly savor it, the Tarot is always there for you.

Chapter 17

Heart Tracks:
Four New Accessory Layouts

Emerson wrote that the great day of the great feast of life comes when our inward eye opens to the unity of things.[88] Working with the Tarot daily and in different ways is one way to foster that opening.

We offer four new spreads for keeping your pulse on various aspects of your relationship, or for examining certain facets when you don't have time to do a complete Tarot for Two. They are also good when you want to establish a daily focus for your work on the project or relationship, or want an update.

The Heart Express

The heart express is your micro-cross for the day. It's your short and quick fix on where you and another are coming from for that day or the challenge each of you can expect to face.

Use the same-size cards to represent you and the other as you did for the original question and Tarot for Two reading. Shuffle or mix your cards, requesting guidance for the day as to your task and your challenge for a specific problem or issue which has already been established. Cut your cards into two piles representing Where am I today? and What's in my way today?

Shuffle or mix the cards representing the other, requesting information as to how his or her task and challenge will interface with your own. Cut the other's deck into two piles, also designating them as Where am I today? and What's in my way today?

Place the top card from the larger deck's Where am I today? stack in card position 1 (see Figure 4) and the top card from the smaller deck's Where am I today? stack in card position 2.

Place the top card from the larger deck's What's in my way today? pile in position 3 and the top card from the smaller deck's What's in my way today? stack in position 4.

---

[88] *Selected Prose and Poetry*, 1969.

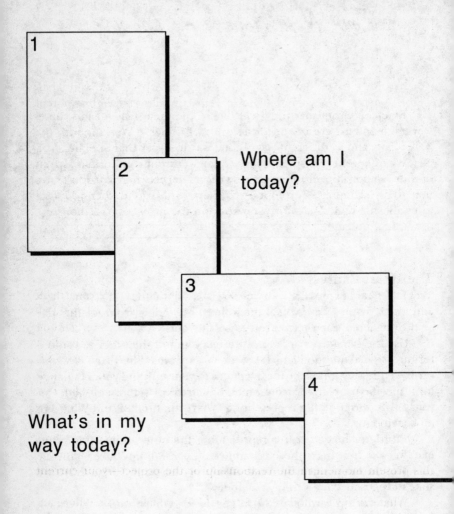

Figure 4
The Heart Express Layout

Interpret the micro-cross as you would the micro-cross for the Tarot for Two spread (see "The Heart of the Matter" in Chapter 11).

The Heartgram

The heartgram can be used anytime you want to determine where your relationship is with respect to five important aspects: you, your challenge, available resources, hidden influences, and the unfolding potential of the relationship.

It can serve as a guidepost, giving you a daily or weekly fix on the status or progress of your Tarotscape relationship. Or it can serve as a quick guideline on the major elements of a new project or relationship prior to doing a complete Tarot for Two layout.

If you are monitoring the progress of a continuing project or relationship, and have already completed a Tarot for Two, you do not necessarily need to ask an additional question. Use the same-size cards to represent each of you as you did with the original question.

On the other hand, if this is your first spread, then you need to carefully consider and formulate your question (see Chapter 10, "Ask and You Shall Receive"), as well as decide which deck represents you and which represents the other (see Chapter 10, "Who's on Top?").

Shuffle the two decks. As you shuffle your deck, focus on gaining insight for your day's work on your question. When you shuffle the deck representing the other person, focus on gaining information as to his or her present position with respect to the question.

Deal the cards from the top of each deck. As with the Tarot for Two layout, the larger card goes on the bottom and the smaller card on top of it (see figure 5).

The first position (Where am I today?, cards 1 and 2) represents each of you today. It answers the question of who and how you are at this present moment in the relationship or the project—your current state of focus.

What's in my way today? cards (3 and 4) are laid across Where am I today? cards to form a cross. This is the micro-cross of the Tarot for Two layout. In the Heartgram layout, the challenges that will face each of you *today* with respect to the relationship or the question issue are shown. Interpret this cross in the same way as the micro-cross of the Tarot for Two spread (see "The Heart of the Matter" in Chapter 11).

Cards 5 and 6—What are my skills?—show inner or outer resources you and your other will have to draw on if you tackle work related to the question or issue. Look for the kinds of skills each of you bring and

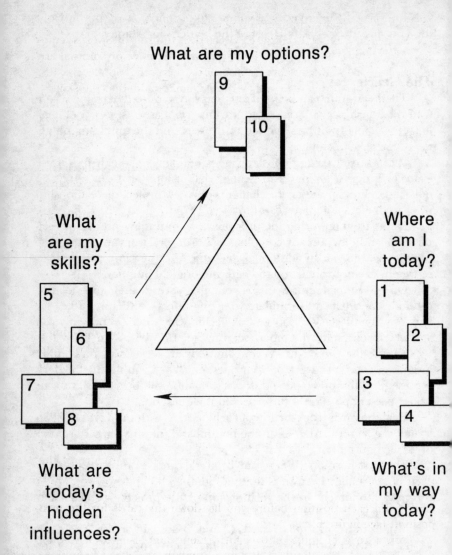

Figure 5
The Heartgram Layout

whether or not they complement one another or are at odds.

Remember, mental skills are reflected in the suit of Swords, emotional with Cups, physical with Pentacles, and intuitive or spiritual are represented by Wands. Major Arcana cards represent high-level skills, skills elevated to new levels, or a spiritual element added to the skill.

Cards 7 and 8—What are today's hidden influences?—are laid across What are my skills? cards to form a second cross. They reflect aspects of the issue or question which you are ignoring or which will be activated by others during the day.

Court cards may represent persons in lines of authority above you, such as foremen (Pages), managers (Knights), or top executives (Queens and Kings).

Finally, cards 9 and 10 answer the question, "What are my options?" They can reflect the unfolding potential of the day as a result of your efforts. They may also point to possible directions that will be opened to you, or opportunities you should be ready to spot and act on.

The Heart's Creation

This spread is a good one to use anytime you are contemplating a new project or relationship. It is also appropriate to use when you want to "dialogue" with your project. Its major purpose is not so much to give you guidance as it is to broaden or sharpen your perspective.

The spread is laid out in the shape of a diamond, one symbol of the creative mind. The cards for each position do not touch, although the pairs in each position do overlap.

Select the two decks to represent each of you, or you and your project. Shuffle each deck, requesting insight into the nature of the project or relationship. Draw from the top of each deck. Place the cards from the large deck first, with the smaller cards on top. Interpret the cards from each position before you lay down the cards for the next position (see figure 6).

Vision cards (1 and 2) show your present state of mind. If you are seeking information about an ongoing situation or project, they show what's happening. If you are contemplating a new project or relationship, Vision cards show the attitudes or skills two people will bring to it. They signal the status of your idea and suggest limits or boundaries you need to consider, as well as ways you may be unduly limiting your respective visions.

What's working and not working appears in The Analysis position (cards 3 and 4). These cards also show what needs to be done next or

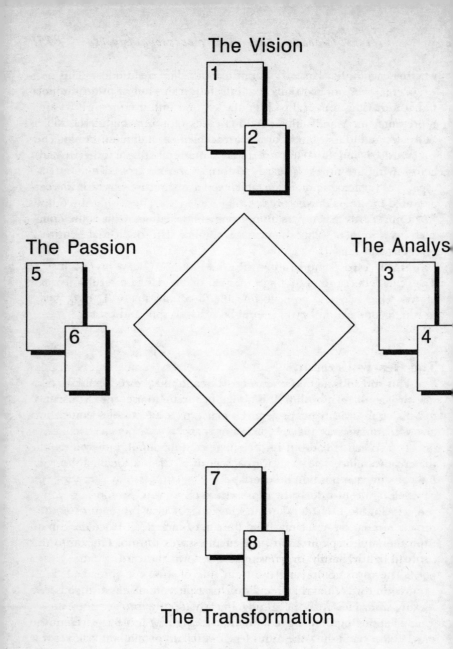

Figure 6
The Heart's Creation Layout

what needs to be clarified or adjusted (actions or attitudes). This position can give you information about the cycles of your project or relationship if it is already ongoing.

Passion cards (5 and 6) highlight the emotional attitudes as well as skills and abilities you have available for the project or relationship. They also can point out sources of inspiration—spiritual or otherwise—or information you may not have fully recognized or utilized.

The Transformation (7 and 8) is an integrative position. Perceptions from the previous cards come together to reflect what the output of your work will be if you attend to their guidelines. This is the culmination of your physical, intellectual, emotional, and spiritual efforts.

Dagaz: A Melding Rune

This is a spread of enlightenment and synthesis. It is laid out in the shape of the dagaz rune, ⋈, which represents the flash of realization or coming together that occurs after mental effort.

If you tend to classify things in opposites, dagaz is the melding process, the spontaneous insight that occurs when you merge two extremes and understand their position as part of a greater whole rather than as distinct entities. It is the coming together of the pieces into a gestalt.

The dagaz spread is good to use after you have put in some effort on your question or issue, and especially when you are at a stalemate or impasse. Because it is a very personal reading about your role in the relationship or issue, it is the only spread in this book which uses one deck, your own personal deck. And the reading is only done for you personally, not for the other. It is a message to you alone.

Dagaz is a turning point, an awakening. Dagaz represents both the truth seeker and the true seeker. Such a one is likely to receive both spiritual and inspirational (inspired) messages. Do not enter into this spread lightly, hastily, or irreverently.

The cards comprising the right side of the rune spread (1, 2, 3) represent the archetypal masculine, that aspect of ourselves which is able to organize and to think logically, linearly (see figure 7).

The cards on the left side of the rune figure (4, 5, 6) represent the archetypal feminine. When this type of archetypal thinking or energy is active, the resources of our unconscious and our inner wisdom are available to us.

To begin the dagaz spread, shuffle the deck once, holding in your mind a request for enlightenment. Divide the deck into six piles from right to left—from linear to global thinking, from logical thinking to

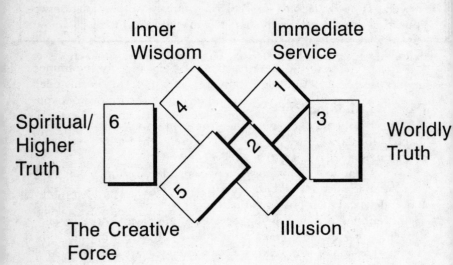

Figure 7
The Dagaz Layout

wisdom. Name them as you lay each one down: Immediate Service, Illusion, Worldly Truth, Inner Wisdom, Creative Force, Higher Truth.

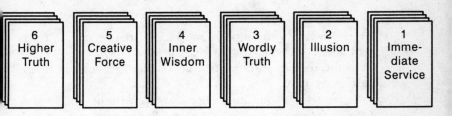

| 6 Higher Truth | 5 Creative Force | 4 Inner Wisdom | 3 Wordly Truth | 2 Illusion | 1 Imme-diate Service |

Cards from the first pile on the right are the source for the Immediate Service position. Shuffle or otherwise mix the cards in this pile, requesting information on the kind and quality of service or work you need to bring into the situation, the kind of service that will make a difference or will infuse the situation with new vitality. Place the top card in position 1 of the dagaz spread.

The second position offers information as to an illusion that is blocking progress, possibly the beliefs you are operating from. Mix the cards from the second pile, requesting insight into your illogical thinking or your incorrect perceptions. Place the top card in position 2, taking care that it touches the bottom of the position 1 card.

The third position, Worldly Truth, is the culmination of the prayer or meditation stimulated by the first two positions. It presents a lower truth or insight that can help you move forward in the relationship or issue. Do not be surprised if it is something you have been considering or an insight that has been playing around at the edge of your awareness.

Mix the cards from the third pile as you request truth or clarity that will unblock your impasse. Place the top card in position 3 so that its inner corners touch or overlap the edges of the first two cards.

Information to fill the fourth position, Inner Wisdom, is stimulated and shaped by the process of drawing and attending to the first three cards and positions. Do not ask for Inner Wisdom (draw the fourth-position cards) until you are satisfied you fully understand and accept the internal reorganization that the cards from the first three positions require. Take time to consider their information before you select the next three cards.

When you are ready to proceed, mix the cards from the fourth stack, requesting that the voice of your inner or higher wisdom make itself known at this time. Place the top card in position 4 so that it touches the edges of the cards in positions 1 and 2. Often this card indicates the structure or discipline needed to carry out the reorganization required by the first three cards.

The fifth position represents the creative force that will be released by:

a. the correct service

b. the resolution of the process specified in the first three cards tempered by Inner Wisdom guidance.

It also shows the creative knowledge or action you have to draw upon, your creative reserves.

Mix the cards from your fifth pile, asking for awareness of the creative energies you need to activate or that will be activated as a result of the interworking of the first three cards. Place the top card in position 5 so its bottom touches the cards in positions 2 and 4 and so it is directly aligned across from position 1.

The sixth position is the culmination of the forces activated by the reading. It is the revelation of a higher, possibly spiritual truth that will need to be carried into your relationship or the issue question.

Mix the cards from your sixth (last) pile, asking that higher wisdom, the truth that can create wholeness, be opened to you.

Place the top card in position 6 so its inner corners touch or overlap the edges of the cards in positions 4 and 5.

When you understand the import of your dagaz reading or commit to taking time later to reflect on it, thank whatever higher deities or forces you believe in for their input into the reading.

Chapter 18

Heart Singers:
A Mandala Growth Ritual

That unique combination of ritual, healing, performance, and art that creates the Navajo sand painting is one of our great Native American traditions. Shamans or medicine men who know the process for chanting each special ritual and creating its accompanying painting are called singers.

Thus we refer to the two of you who participate in the mandala growth ritual and create a Tarot mandala as heart singers.

The mandala growth ritual serves as a ceremony to mark the beginning of a significant new phase in the relationship or a new year together. It takes about one and a half to two hours to complete and should not be used more than once a year.

Materials Needed:

The following materials should be selected with colors and shapes that appeal to you or have symbolic meaning within your relationship:

1. Two decks of cards.
2. Water that has been left standing in a covered container in sunlight and moonlight for twenty-four hours and is now placed in an open, shallow container. Abalone shells or bowls special to you are nice.
3. Two candles—color and size determined by partners—and holders for them.
4. Matches to light the candles.
5. Edible seeds, such as sunflower seeds, to represent the fullness of nature.
6. One copy of the Growth Mandala Form.
7. Paper and pencil to record any card meanings you want to jot down. As you progress through the ritual, you may find it helpful to record impressions and feelings you want to remember throughout the year or want to discuss more fully near the end of the ritual.

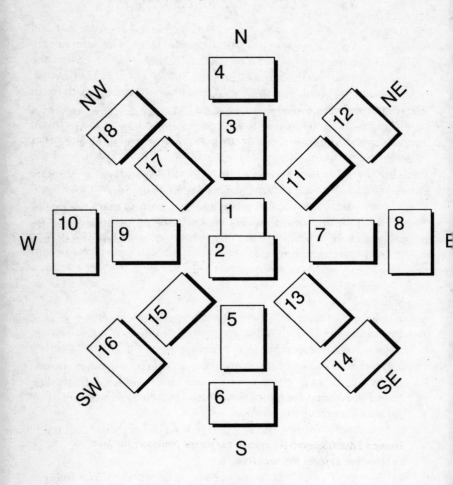

Figure 8
The Growth Mandala

After each position, take no more than ten minutes to discuss the implications of the cards for your relationship. If you need more time, make notes and continue your discussion later. Long discussions break the continuity of the ritual.

Decks for this ritual spread can be of any size as they are not laid on top of each other, except to form the center cross. The woman constructs the inner circle; the man constructs the outer circle. Orient the spread so its north or uppermost position is laid down in your actual, physical north. The couple sit facing one another on the north-south line, the man facing south, the woman facing north.

The first two cards form the center of the mandala. Subsequent cards form the four directions or anchors of the mandala in the order of north (top), south (bottom), east, and west. The remainder of the cards are placed between them to build the mandala in a clockwise direction. All cards are selected or turned over with the left hand and placed in position with the right hand.

There are nine pairs of positions in the mandala, 9 being the number of completion and wisdom. Eighteen cards are used to construct the mandala. Not only does 18 symbolize the path we must travel toward enlightenment, but its integers added together total 9 ($8 + 1 = 9$), a triple completion.

Beginning the Growth Mandala Ritual:

After you have assembled your materials, open the growth mandala ritual with the following Invocation:

Man Heart Singer: *We request the wisdom and powers of the ages to guide us in creating this mandala.*

Woman Heart Singer: *We beseech the sacred powers of the four directions to support the mandala.*

Man Heart Singer: *We call upon the four elements to add to our understanding of our place in the cosmos.*

Woman Heart Singer: *We ask that this mandala enlighten us.*

Together: *We dedicate this mandala to our continued growth and healing.*

Each person shuffles his or her own deck. With your left hand, fan or spread the cards face down. Select a card from your individual fans to be placed in what will become the center cross of the mandala (see figure 8). Place it with your right hand.

Leave the remainder of your cards face down, fanned out.

The man's card (No. 1)—or whoever represents the male element in the relationship—is placed upright (north-south). The woman's or female card (2) is placed across it horizontally (east-west).

Together they represent the union of the spiritual and the earthly, as well as your own union as a couple. They present your inner states of being and commitment as you begin the ceremonial spread and finish this particular cycle of your relationship.

Facing one another and touching hands, take three simultaneous deep breaths, pacing yourselves together. Select a card from your respective fans and place it simultaneously in the north (air) position, above the central cross.

The woman places her card upright in position 3 to begin forming the inner mandala. The man places his card sideways in position 4 to begin forming the outer mandala. This upright position for the inner mandala and sideways position for the outer mandala continue throughout the ceremony.

Cards in the north position present your exterior facade, some element of the mask you show to the world and possibly to one another.

Using the water, anoint each other on the forehead, eyelids, nose, lips, and ears. Select a card from your fan and place it in the south (water) position, below the two central cards and aligned with the first two cards. The woman places her card in position 5, the man in position 6.

The water position reflects your inner visions, your daytime dreams about yourself and/or the relationship.

Before drawing a card for the fire position, each of your lights a candle and hands it to the other, accepting it with your right hand. Place your candles in holders. Select and place your cards in the east (7 and 8) position of the mandala.

The fire position is one of new beginnings. Cards in this position can show fresh attitudes you have for this year or phase of your relationship, or new possibilities to consider adding to the relationship.

Feed one another a few seeds, then select your cards and place them in the west (earth) position (9 and 10) of the mandala. Earth cards denote completion and fulfillment; where you have come from; something that ends with the present phase or cycle of your relationship.

Reshuffle the remaining cards and with your left hand divide them into four piles from right to left, representing the cycles of Choice, Creation, Attainment, and Cosmos, respectively.

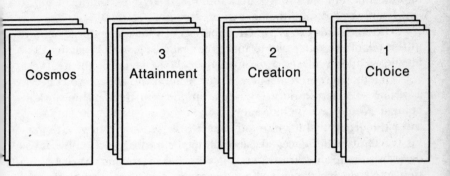

4	3	2	1
Cosmos	Attainment	Creation	Choice

When you have turned over and placed your card from each pile according to the directions that follow, do not restack the piles. That will come later.

Shuffle or mix the Choice cycle cards, requesting insight about what you need to learn from each other during the coming year or how you can serve as resources for one another. With your left hand, turn over your respective top cards and place them (with your right hand) in the northeast (11 and 12) positions.

Choice cycle cards offer information about your direction for the year; alternatives you need to consider; choices you need to make now to enter a new phase. They also can show what the other has to teach you.

Shuffle or mix the Creation cycle cards, requesting knowledge related to what you need to do together (work, projects, goals) during the coming year. Turn over your top cards, placing them in the southeast (13 and 14) positions.

By their suit qualities, Creation cycle cards suggest the kinds of goals or projects (mental, physical, emotional, intuitive/spiritual) you need to concentrate on. Card meanings and symbology fill in the details.

Shuffle or mix the Attainment cycle cards, requesting insight about what it is possible for you to achieve in the coming year. Turn over and place the top cards in the southwest (15 and 16) positions.

Given the knowledge of what you have to offer one another and what your joint goals or work together will be, the Attainment cycle suggests your achievements from the coming year's work, or, possibly, from work already set in motion.

Shuffle or mix the Cosmic cycle cards, requesting clarity and expanded awareness. Turn over and place the top cards in the northwest (17 and 18) position. The Cosmic cycle position is one of liberation and expansion, renewal and regeneration. It is the cosmos's ultimate gift to you to be used during the next year.

Cosmic cards can represent an aspect of your inner spirit you have liberated or awakened as a result of the mandala growth ritual. It will be your inspiration or special resource, on call for you during the next year.

It also can represent a personal or relationship illusion you need to discard or qualities you need to activate for your relationship work together during the coming year.

If there is anything else you want to discuss about your growth mandala or your experience, take about fifteen minutes to do so now. If you have not done this already, make a record of the mandala so you may refer to it during the year or continue your discussion after closing the ritual.

Closing the Growth Mandala Ritual:

With your right hand, restack the four piles together from left to right, which is the reverse of the order in which you created them. Bow to, and thank, one another to acknowledge your respective contributions to the construction of the mandala. Remove the two center cards and replace them in your decks.

Set aside the Cosmic cycle card so you can place it in some prominent position for the remainder of the day. During the day—and from time to time during the ensuing year—you may wish to meditate on your Cosmic cycle card.

Bow to the four directions to thank them for revealing those patterns of your relationship which you need for growth and healing. Working counterclockwise and beginning with the west position, return the remaining cards to your deck. Extinguish your candles. Sit quietly for a moment to take this experience back into your being and to offer any private devotions of your choosing.

Then, according to your own timing, you may wish to finish your conversations about the mandala or the ritual. At the conclusion of many rituals there is often a party or feasting. You may want to share refreshments at this time, possibly including friends in your celebration.

Please also accept our congratulations and blessings for this new phase of your relationship work.

Appendices:
A Gallery of Resources

Appendix 1
Blank Forms for Recording Layouts

We hope you will reproduce and enlarge the blank forms in Appendix 1 so you will have a supply handy to keep track of any Tarot for Two readings you do. This lets you monitor not only your achievements in learning the techniques described in *The Lovers' Tarot*, but your progress and insight into your relationships as well.

Date _____

P1 _____

P2 _____

Question _____

_____

_____

_____

_____

Where does all this lead?

19 | 20

What do I expect?

18 | 19

What's out there for me?

15 | 16

Who do I think I am?

13 | 14

What else is new?

21 | 22

What's in store for me?

9 | 10

What are my options?
Where am I?

11 | 12

1 | 2 | 4
3

What's in my way?

5 | 6

Where have I been?

What's been happening?

7 | 8

‹TAROTSCAPE›

Heart Express Record

Name P-1_____ Date _____

Name P-2 _____

Question _____

```
┌─────────────────┐
│ 1               │
│                 │
│                 │        Where am I
│   ┌─────────────┴──┐     today?
│   │ 2              │
│   │                │
└───┤                │
    │   ┌────────────┴──────────┐
    │   │ 3                     │
    └───┤                       │
        │                       │
        │        ┌──────────────┴──────────┐
        │        │ 4                       │
What's in my     │                         │
way today?       │                         │
        └────────┤                         │
                 │                         │
                 └─────────────────────────┘
```

Where am I today?

What's in my way today?

Heartgram Record

Name P-1 _____ Date _____

Name P-2 _____

Question _____

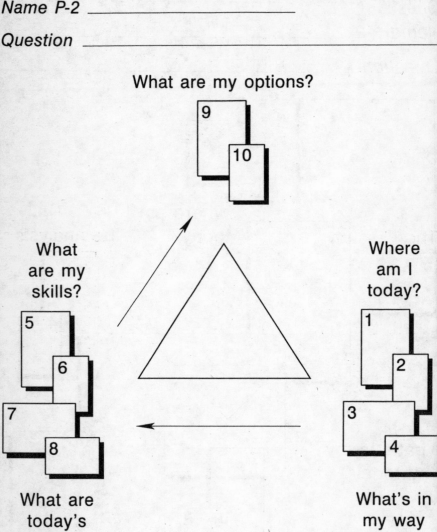

What are my options?

What are my skills?

Where am I today?

What are today's hidden influences?

What's in my way today?

Heart's Creation Record

Name P-1 _____   Date _____

Name P-2 _____

Question _____

The Vision

1

2

The Passion

5

6

The Analysis

3

4

The Transformation

7

8

Dagaz Record

Name P-1 _____ Date _____

Name P-2 _____

Question _____

Inner
Wisdom

Immediate
Service

Spiritual/
Higher
Truth

Worldl
Truth

The Creative
Force

Illusion

Comments and Insights: _____

_____

_____

_____

_____

Record
Mandala Growth Ritual

Name P-1 _____ *Date* _____

Name P-2 _____

Question _____

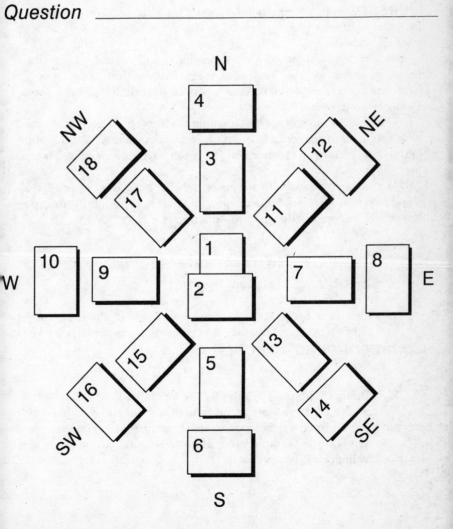

Blank Interpretive Question Worksheets for Tarot for Two Heartprints

The questions presented in Chapter 11, which you should consider for each heartprint pair, are reproduced as Appendix 2, with spaces for your responses.

Duplicating the material in Appendix 2, and keeping the appropriate questions in front of you as you turn over the cards for each heartprint, will remind you of ideas you need to consider and allow you to record your answers.

Certainly, when you are first learning the Tarot for Two, take all the time you need to answer each question and understand each heartprint before you turn over another pair, for each successive pair builds on preceding pairs.

If you need more help in answering the questions, Appendix 3 shows how one of our students answered them for the sample Tarotscape shown in Chapter 11 and again in Appendix 4.

WHERE AM I?

(Cards 1 and 2)

1. If there are people on the cards, what is their status, age, sex, activity? Do you think they represent you or others involved in the question?

2. If there are no people, what do the animals (if any), or objects, on the cards indicate as prominent in your mind at present? Use Chapter 8 symbology to check whether they represent action or introspection, cooperation or isolation, loving or hostile feelings.

3. What do the people, animals, objects, or activities suggest about the attitudes, opinions, and expectations you are bringing into the current situation?

4. What do the cards suggest about your respective levels of mental functioning, including education and life experience and their compatibility, or incompatibility, for your interaction?

5. What strengths or limitations that affect the question does each of you bring to the relationship?

6. What do the cards suggest about your sexual activities?

WHAT'S IN MY WAY?

(Cards 3 and 4)

1. What kind of problem is it? Is the nature of the challenge mental (Swords), emotional (Cups), physical (Pentacles), or intuitive/ spiritual (Wands)? Is it archetypal (Major Arcana) or mundane (Minor Arcana)?

2. How do other people or outside influences shown on the cards seem to be helping or interfering?

3. What resources or support does each have to help the other in facing the challenge?

4. Compare the challenges. Do you each recognize and acknowledge your own challenge and that of the other?

WHERE HAVE I BEEN?

(Cards 5 and 6)

1. What do the cards show about the mental, intuitive/spiritual, emotional, or physical development each has experienced?

2. Do people, objects, and activities on the card point out shared or conflicting values?

3. What common experiences are shown?

4. Has the issue raised by the question come up before? Is there a repeating pattern here?

5. Does the presence of court cards reveal past experiences or attitudes about authority or leadership?

6. Do past sexual experiences influence the question?

WHAT'S BEEN HAPPENING?

(Cards 7 and 8)

1. Are your recent-past events of a mental, emotional, intuitive/spiritual, or physical nature.

2. How do they differ between you?

3. Have recent-past events changed the mood of the relationship?

4. Has there been a shift in dominance or passivity of one or the other?

5. Has a recent sexual interaction influenced the issue?

6. Has a third party, or other influence, come into the picture?

WHAT'S IN STORE FOR ME?
(Cards 9 and 10)

1. Will your near-future events be of a mental, intuitive/spiritual, emotional, or physical nature?

2. Will they be caused by an outside influence, or by one or both of you?

3. Will you respond actively or passively?

4. Which of you will be most affected by the events?

5. Are these expected events, or is there a surprise in store for one or both of you?

WHAT ARE MY OPTIONS?
(Cards 11 and 12)

1. Is the direction or opportunity of a mental, emotional, intuitive/spiritual, or physical nature?

2. Do people on the cards indicate a shift in active/passive attitudes?

3. Are new avenues for growth shown?

4. Do the cards suggest possibilities for resolving any sexual conflict, if appropriate?

WHO DO I THINK I AM?
(Cards 13 and 14)

1. What part does your self-view play in creating the question or situation?

2. Is your self-view consistent with your current behavior or your problem-solving approach?

3. How is each one's self-view, including sexual attitudes, similar to or different from the other's?

WHAT'S OUT THERE FOR ME?
(Cards 15 and 16)

1. Are there outside influences, communication, or information which can be utilized?

2. Are the influences shown on the cards common to both of you?

3. How will each person react to these influences?

4. Are confrontations or compromises indicated?

5. Are there other people to consider or who may intervene to help?

6. What emotional atmosphere do the symbols on the cards show?

7. Are there external factors that may influence sexual attitudes or behavior?

WHAT DO I EXPECT?
(Cards 17 and 18)

1. Do your expectations involve receiving, getting, doing, serving, or just being?

2. Are your individual expectations compatible or in conflict?

3. How do your expectations relate to the question?

4. Are sexual expectations influencing the question?

5. How do your expectations compare with your Where am I? cards?

WHERE DOES ALL THIS LEAD?
(Cards 19 and 20)

1. What are the similarities or differences in your respective outcomes?

2. What skills or talents are available that you can use to resolve the question?

3. Are they of a mental, emotional, intuitive/spiritual, or physical nature?

4. How do these skills or talents complement, or conflict with, each other?

5. How does the outcome compare with your expectations (What do I expect?)?

WHAT ELSE IS NEW?
(Cards 21 and 22)

1. Does the information on the cards suggest additional resources for implementing the outcome?

2. What emotional, spiritual, or sexual growth possibilities are shown in your What else is new? cards?

Appendix 3

A Student Answers Chapter 11 Heartprints Questions

In order to give our students practice in delving into the bountiful information offered by the cards, we have them create a question, draw an imaginary Tarot for Two layout—just as we have suggested you do— and answer Chapter 11 questions.

Appendix 3 is one student's answers to the cards he drew. His Tarotscape for an imaginary couple was first presented in Chapter 11 as an example of a completed Tarotscape. It is reproduced again in Appendix 4.

His couple's question was: "How can my boyfriend and I make better use of our time together?"

What do you think he discovered about this "couple"?

WHERE AM I?

Nine of Swords & The Empress:
  1. *If there are people on the cards, what is their status, age, sex, activity? Do you think they represent you or others involved in the question?*

    There are people on both cards. Her card shows a person whose sex is not clear, covering his/her face. Is it out of anguish or reflection? On his card is a female of royalty. Need confirmation from couple as to whether the figures represent them.
  2. *If there are no people, what do the animals (if any), or objects, on the cards indicate as prominent in your mind at present?*

    The Empress card says to me isolation, superiority (holding the orb of power), plenty of masculine power (yellow sky), fertility (grains in foreground), and some attendance to stream of consciousness (water in background). There is also a potential for growth (the number 3).

    The preponderance of black in the Nine of Swords suggests the female is an "earthy" woman with a lot of power she is not recognizing. If she is experiencing anguish (perhaps about the question), she is, nevertheless, coming from a place of security (bed and bedspread). Passion (the roses), receptivity (blue), and intellect (yellow) seem about balanced. Two figures on the base of the bed (the two persons?) seem to be one active and one passive. Perhaps they represent the problems of the couple not yet made clearly apparent, or a hunch she has that is not fully formulated.

3. *What do the people, animals, objects, or activities suggest about the attitudes, opinions, and expectations you are bringing into the current situation?*

    Both seem to be somewhat isolated from the other—he coming from a place of aloofness and feeling more powerful; she not recognizing her role, or her capabilities, in the issue at hand.

4. *What do the cards suggest about your respective levels of mental functioning, including education and life experience, and their compatibility, or incompatibility, for your interaction?*

    He is of a "rank" higher than she (either in reality or by his own perception). She probably worries more about the issue than he does.

5. *What strengths or limitations that affect the question does each of you bring to the relationship?*

    If both play into it, his feelings of superiority could contribute to looking down on her. On the other hand, he obviously comes from a place of comfort and success, and that could give him the emotional stamina to deal with their problem if she brings it up (female came for reading, not male). He has the capacity to be more nurturing than he has been, or than she has allowed. She has untapped or unrecognized resources to draw upon for strength. Both are in a good place to begin a new level of interaction (3 and 9). She clearly is calling for a refocus or a reevaluation of their goals as a couple.

6. *What do the cards suggest about your sexual activities?*

    She has a somewhat masculine orientation (Swords), with the ability to analyze and evaluate. She may have some sexual conflicts. He is nurturing and sensitive in his sexual attitudes (The Empress). This could make him a very empathic companion or perhaps be seen by her as a little too sensitive and not decisive enough. His sexual vitality may help her in resolving any sexual conflicts. He should be a good complement for her.

WHAT'S IN MY WAY?

Knight of Pentacles & Six of Cups:

1. *What kind of problem is it? Is the nature of the challenge mental (Swords), emotional (Cups), physical (Pentacles), or intuitive/spiritual (Wands)? Is it archetypal (Major Arcana) or mundane (Minor Arcana)?*

    The challenge appears to be largely intellectual (yellow) for both, with some emotional qualities (Cups): moments of openness and insight (white flowers) on his part, and reflection (silver on the armor) and flexibility (Pentacles) on her part.

2. *How do other people or outside influences shown on the cards seem to be helping or interfering?*

    Her challenge is not with outside influences, but rather is to be persistent, to stick to her principles, i.e., to draw upon her masculine aspects, yet at the same time to balance that with her intuitive understanding of her boyfriend and their relationship. However, she needs to resist carrying the burden of making the change (horse) and to approach the whole issue with caution (yellow).

    [Note: We would have focused on the "new ground plowed," which suggests there needs to be a new way to handle the situation. New ideas need to be planted. The black horse might also represent the boyfriend; and she needs to move him in the direction she wants to go.—*The Authors*]

    His challenge is to not let his memories—possibly those of his relationship with his mother (older woman)—interfere with what his girlfriend is asking.

    [Note: Our student's perception of the smaller figure as an older woman on this card is an unusual response. Usually this figure is interpreted as a female child receiving a gift of flowers.—*The Authors*]

3. *What resources or support does each have to help the other in facing the challenge?*

    He can draw upon and show his emotions (Cups = love, sensuality) to indicate his support of and involvement with her. Her principles will help her take a stand (Knight of Pentacles) and hang in there as he works through his old memories.

4. *Compare the challenges. Do you each recognize and acknowledge your own challenge and that of the other?*

    They are both working in their minds about this issue.

There is some emotion with it and they need to add physical activity.

Need feedback from actual client to answer whether or not they recognize this.

Commentary on the micro-cross (the situation that prompts the reading):
   She is calling for and ready for change in the relationship, but may be ignoring the timing of her sexual nature, which requires slow development for her to feel deeply. Although he is presently in a creative, nurturing frame of mind, old memories keep him from achieving as much harmony with her as his capacity indicates, mentally and possibly sexually. Her persistence raises the issue (initiates the problem) and keeps it alive. But that energy needs to be focused toward reaching a solution so it brings harmony rather than conflict.

WHERE HAVE I BEEN?

Three of Wands & Nine of Swords:
   1. *What do the cards show about the mental, intuitive/spiritual, emotional, or physical development each has experienced?*
      She has probably entered into past relationships—or into this one, depending on how long it has been ongoing—with a great deal of enthusiasm (Wands) and hope for growth together (Wands).
      He may have wrestled with the same issues, possibly in a past relationship, that she is presently wrestling with (duplicate card, Nine of Swords). This creates empathy on his part.
   2. *Do people, objects, and activities on the cards point out shared or conflicting values?*
      I don't see any indication of values in the cards.
      [Note: In the Three of Wands, she may be deriving her values from observing others (watching the ships go by) and the way they do things.—*The Authors*]
   3. *What common experiences are shown?*
      In the past both have experienced a lot of earthy passion (black on Nine of Swords, red robe on Three of Wands), security (bed and spread; green shawl), growth (3 and 9), and isolation (single figure in each card).
   4. *Has the issue raised by the question come up before? Is there a repeating pattern here?*

He has certainly experienced the issue she brings to the reading (duplicate Nine of Swords). I see no repeating pattern here except a lot of yellow on her card, which may indicate she has had a similar challenge in the past.

5. *Does the presence of court cards reveal past experiences or attitudes about authority or leadership?*

No court cards present.

6. *Do past sexual experiences influence the question?*

She has begun sexual exploration and discovery (3), but her feminine nature is not as yet fully developed (3; Wands suit). At this point he may be too analytical or critical in comparing their present sexual relationship with past ones.

WHAT'S BEEN HAPPENING?

Page of Cups & Four of Swords:

1. *Are your recent-past events of a mental, emotional, intuitive/spiritual, or physical nature?*

Hers have been emotional; his have been mental.

2. *How do they differ between you?*

She's probably been more aware of what she was feeling about their situation, while he has been pondering it—perhaps with a logical approach. It would be important to know whether his "thinking" approach is his attempt to balance her emotionality with respect to this particular issue, or whether it is characteristic of their problem-solving style as a couple, i.e., is this what usually happens?

3. *Have recent-past events changed the mood of the relationship?*

She has been reviewing the nature of their relationship (blue; Page = 11) and her feelings about it and him (Cups). He also (Swords), but from the point of view of trying to define the relationship or where he is in it (4).

4. *Has there been a shift in dominance or passivity of one or the other?*

From distant past to recent past, she has come to rely less on intellect and more on intuition (blue and water). He has made a shift from intuitive to intellectual (yellow on Four of Swords), and both shifts are reflected in their Where am I? cards (hers: bedspread on Nine of Swords; his: yellow sky on The Empress).

5. *Has a recent sexual interaction influenced the issue?*

She has recently had a new sexual experience or has overcome a sexual block. This has expanded her imagination and increased her sensitivity. As a result, she has a new insight into sexual possibilities. He, on the other hand, is in a place of sexual introspection and healing and is not as focused on sexual activity or experimentation as she is.

6. *Has a third party, or other influence, come into the picture?*

Not a third party exactly, but he seems to be wrestling so much between a physical union and a spiritual union (gray) in the distant and recent past that I wonder (a) if he is healing from a past relationship, (b) if he is considering becoming a priest, or (c) if one of his hang-ups is getting his caring and his feelings about money mixed up in his relationships with women, or with this particular woman.

WHAT'S IN STORE FOR ME?

Ace of Cups & Justice:

1. *Will your near-future events be of a mental, intuitive/spiritual, emotional, or physical nature?*

Near-future events indicate a profound (Justice) reconciliation (gray; Eucharist) of a most emotional (blue water; Cups) or passionate (red robe) kind.

2. *Will they be caused by an outside influence, or by one or both of you?*

Hers will be prompted by an outside (hand) influence, possibly of a spiritual or meditational nature, possibly by someone who is a Pisces (blue = color of Pisces). His is an inner process of balancing.

3. *Will you respond actively or passively?*

They will respond actively. She will open up and offer her feelings, begin to trust—with the result that sex will be more satisfactory for her. He, in turn, will seek to achieve a balance in the relationship for them as a couple and for himself as an individual.

4. *Which of you will be most affected by the events?*

Both will be strongly affected (Ace of Cups = intense feelings; Major Arcana for him; about the same amount of yellow in each card).

5. *Are these expected events, or is there a surprise in store for one or both of you?*

> Probably a most enlightening (lily) and satisfying (dove) surprise or insight (hand, clouds) for her. He expects things to be balanced.

WHAT ARE MY OPTIONS?

Ten of Cups & Temperance:

1. *Is the direction or opportunity of a mental, emotional, intuitive/spiritual, or physical nature?*

> Hers is an emotional (Cups) opportunity. His will be more dramatic—at least for him—than hers (Major Arcana), even though it will be one of working toward balance.

2. *Do people on the cards indicate a shift in active/passive attitudes?*

> She continues to rely on intuition and trust her feelings (blue), while he begins to allow more of that (blue water) back into his way of interacting. He has clearly come to a resolution of issues between them (Temperance card; gray) and an appreciation of her spiritual experience/insight.

3. *Are new avenues for growth shown?*

> Yes, especially for her (10 = completion of an old cycle and beginning a new one). He could experience new balance and equanimity in his life as a whole through their love.

4. *Do the cards suggest possibilities for resolving any sexual conflict, if appropriate?*

> Both cards indicate a striving for harmony and balance. Her unfolding experiences and understandings will deepen their sexual commitment to one another. He will come to some balance between sexual memories or fantasies and reality and will become more considerate of her ideas and needs.

WHO DO I THINK I AM?

The Devil & Nine of Wands:

1. *What part does your self-view play in creating the question or situation?*

> She misunderstands the nature of his wounds and does not realize how much they create distance and the lack of quality time. His wounds help him maintain a defensive, protective

stance and not work to get closer, more intimate during their time together.

2. *Is your self-view consistent with your current behavior or your problem-solving approach?*

His current behavior is especially consistent with his approach to problem solving as depicted in his cards in the cross. However, he sees himself as having more access to his unconscious/intuition (blue) than cards in the cross reveal.

She shows a possibility of acting helpless (being in bed alone on the Nine of Swords; being chained in The Devil card).

3. *How is each one's self-view, including sexual attitudes, similar to or different from the other's?*

She sees herself as fearful and sexually conservative, but able to laugh at illusions once she identifies them. He sees himself as resourceful and prepared, yet cautious because he has been wounded (bandage). He may be oversensitive to sexual rejection. They each have different perceptions of their abilities to overcome their fears.

WHAT'S OUT THERE FOR ME?

Seven of Swords & Three of Swords:

1. *Are there outside influences, communication, or information which can be utilized?*

An opportunity will present itself to successfully (3; 7) "cut through" illusions which have sustained them and their conflict about the present issue.

2. *Are the influences shown on the cards common to both of you?*

Yes, both will experience mental stimulation and action (Swords for each); however, hers will provide assurance, his doubt.

3. *How will each person react to these influences?*

She will use her intellect to analyze and resolve the issues and achieve equilibrium (yellow; 7). She will struggle but triumph.

He also will employ logic and reason, but will be more reticent and fearful than she—maybe even withdraw temporarily—to reconcile (gray) their differences and/or his personal illusions (clouds)—possibly about her, relationships, or women in general. He will get clear about his love for her (red heart).

4. *Are confrontations or compromises indicated?*

Confrontation, yes (Swords for both), and for both a successful completion of the struggle (3; 7).

5. *Are there other people to consider or who may intervene to help?*

There certainly is a male in the situation for her. Because this is an exercise, it cannot be determined whether the male figure on the card is the boyfriend or another.

6. *What emotional atmosphere do the symbols on the cards show?*

These cards show more of an intellectual atmosphere (both Swords; gray on the Three of Swords; yellow on the Seven of Swords).

7. *Are there external factors that may influence sexual attitudes or behavior?*

She may have an opportunity for experimentation with other sex partners. He, in turn, likely will be frustrated by her changing attitude, which will cause him to reevaluate his role in the relationship.

WHAT DO I EXPECT?

The Hierophant & Ten of Swords:

1. *Do your expectations involve receiving, getting, doing, serving, or just being?*

Hers involve listening to herself and teaching him. His include being with himself and internally reorganizing his thoughts and feelings, possibly receiving from her.

2. *Are your individual expectations compatible or in conflict?*

They are compatible.

3. *How do your expectations relate to the question?*

He will have to work through some issues which frighten him before he can receive from her. She will need to use her sensitivity to be alert to when he is ready to receive from her.

4. *Are sexual expectations influencing the question?*

She expects to outwardly conform to a restricted pattern of sexual behavior, yet hopes sex will be a spiritual as well as a physical experience. He is devastated when she does not share in his feelings of sex as recreation and fears her attitudes may erode his sexual focus.

5. *How do your expectations compare with your Where am I? cards?*

She can expect to recognize the power she was not recognizing with the Nine of Swords. He will feel less isolated (The Empress) after his internal struggle.

WHERE DOES ALL THIS LEAD?

Queen of Cups & Eight of Wands:

1. *What are the similarities or differences in your respective outcomes?*

   The outcome is different for each of them. She is involved with emotions and he is concerned with different ideas about things to do together.

2. *What skills or talents are available that you can use to resolve the question?*

   She has emotional skills and sensitivity. He brings enthusiasm, the push for growth, and ideas for what to do.

3. *Are they of a mental, emotional, intuitive/spiritual, or physical nature?*

   Hers are emotional (Cups); his, intuitive/spiritual (Wands).

4. *How do these skills or talents complement or conflict with each other?*

   They should complement one another very well.

5. *How does the outcome compare with your expectations (What do I expect?)?*

   She will still be more emotionally expressive than he, but as her understanding and sensitivity become more sophisticated, she will appear less obvious as a teacher and more as the sexually mature companion.

   He wanted personal reorganization, and as a result of his conscious efforts to achieve that, he will have more choices open to him, more ideas available.

WHAT ELSE IS NEW?

The Fool & Queen of Wands:

1. *Does the information on the cards suggest additional resources for implementing the outcome?*

   She will become less fearful in her choices, more joyful and trusting—lighten up—while he will become more open and revealing. Still, as her world and her life expand (mountains), she will be alert (dog) for ways to spur him away from his mental/emotional independence (black cat).

2. *What emotional, spiritual, or sexual growth possibilities are shown in your What else is new? cards?*

For her possibilities, see answer to Question #1.

The possibility is certainly there for him to grow and achieve insight (sunflower), to become more domestic, achieve integration (crown), and become more stable (throne) in the relationship.

Tarot for Two Interpretation Created Using Worksheets 1–3

Throughout this book, we have referred to a layout drawn by one of our students after he devised an imaginary couple with an imaginary question. This is one of the best ways to learn and practice Tarot for Two techniques.

Appendix 4 contains our student's completed worksheets for his couple. If, as we suggested, you drew this same Tarotscape and used it to practice completing the worksheets in Chapter 13, you now have a basis for comparing your answers.

Our student was a beginning Tarot reader. So are you. Use the completed worksheets in this appendix as resources and guides, but not as the definitive word. Undoubtedly our student would complete them differently now that he has had more practice, as, indeed, will you with more experience.

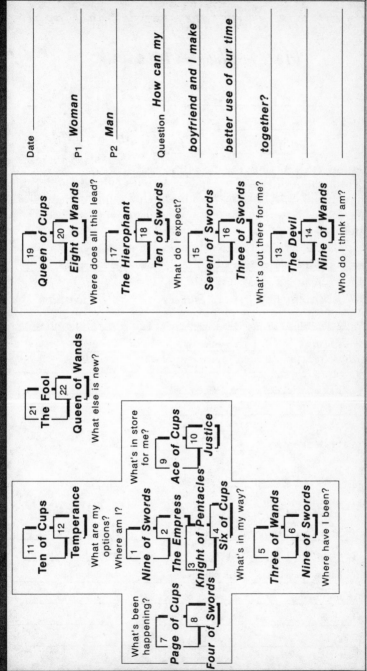

Date _____

P1 *Woman*

P2 *Man*

Question *How can my*

boyfriend and I make

better use of our time

together?

TAROTSCAPE

Queen of Cups | 19
Eight of Wands | 20
Where does all this lead?

The Hierophant | 17
Ten of Swords | 18
What do I expect?

Seven of Swords | 15
Three of Swords | 16
What's out there for me?

The Devil | 13
Nine of Wands | 14
Who do I think I am?

The Fool | 21
Queen of Wands | 22
What else is new?

Ten of Cups | 11
Temperance | 12
What are my options?
Where am I?

Nine of Swords | 1
The Empress | 2
What's in store for me?

Ace of Cups | 9
Justice | 10

Knight of Pentacles | 3
Six of Cups | 4
What's in my way?

Page of Cups | 7
Four of Swords | 8
What's been happening?

Three of Wands | 5
Nine of Swords | 6
Where have I been?

Worksheet #1

The Heartbeat of the Relationship

Person 1   Woman

Person 2   Man

Date

Question   How can my boyfriend and I make better

use of our time together?

WHERE AM I?

Cards: P1 Nine of Swords   P2 The Empress
(Major Arcana III)

Meanings	*Stances*	*Heartlink*
1. Introspection; reevaluation.	She is thinking, reevaluating.	He will support her ideas.
2. Creative; nurturing.	He has the capacity to be creative and nurturing.	

WHAT'S IN MY WAY?

Cards: P1 Knight of Pentacles   .   P2 Six of Cups

Meanings	*Stances*	*Heartlink*
3. Overseer; persistent; principled.	She will have to be persistent.	If she is persistent, he will work through past conditioning.
4. Childhood memories; reconciliation; harmony.	He will have to reconcile old memories with the present relationship.	

Worksheet #1 (cont.)

Micro-Cross Statement

The potential for balance and harmony exists if the challenge is not ignored.

For success, she needs to give practical directions (Knight; 12; 1 + 2 = 3). He

needs to resolve discrepancies (6) between his intuition and his emotions—to

examine his conditioning.

WHERE HAVE I BEEN?

Cards: P1 Three of Wands   P2 Nine of Swords

	Meanings	*Stances*	*Heartlink*
5.	Commitment; contemplation; energetic interaction.	She has been committed, albeit with more enthusiasm.	They have worked separately.
6.	Self-appraisal; introspection; reevaluation.	He has worked on himself.	

WHAT'S BEEN HAPPENING?

Cards: P1 Page of Cups   P2 Four of Swords

	Meanings	*Stances*	*Heartlink*
7.	Increased awareness; emotional sensitivity.	Recently she has become more sensitive about their time together.	His withdrawal alerted and concerned her.
8.	Retreat; introspection; healing.	He has withdrawn for self-healing.	

Worksheet #1 (cont.)

WHAT'S IN STORE FOR ME?

Cards: P1 Ace of Cups   P2 Justice (Major Arcana XI)

Meanings	*Stances*	*Heartlink*
9. New aspect of relationship; joy.	She will experience joy and a fresh slant in their relationship.	Both will experience harmony and balance in the relationship.
10. Stability in relationship; balance.	He will come to sense balance and experience a stability within himself and the relationship.	

WHAT ARE MY OPTIONS?

Cards: P1 Ten of Cups   P2 Temperance (Major Arcana XIV)

Meanings	*Stances*	*Heartlink*
11. Fulfillment; success.	She will feel more fulfilled in their time together.	Both will be more satisfied in the relationship.
12. Balance of spiritual and material; modifications.	He will modify his views to achieve a balance for himself.	

Worksheet #1 (cont.)

WHO DO I THINK I AM?

Cards: P1 <u>The Devil (Major Arcana XV)</u> P2 <u>Nine of Wands</u>

Meanings	*Stances*	*Heartlink*
13. <u>Fear; compulsion; seeing through limitations.</u>	<u>She sees herself as fearful but able to see through it.</u>	<u>They both have attitudes that hold them back.</u>
14. <u>Prepared; resourceful; cautious; defensive.</u>	<u>He sees himself as resourceful but careful.</u>	

WHAT'S OUT THERE FOR ME?

Cards: P1 <u>Seven of Swords</u> P2 <u>Three of Swords</u>

Meanings	*Stances*	*Heartlink*
15. <u>Ingenious planning; completion of mental cycle.</u>	<u>Her planning will evoke fear in him, but she will draw upon her ingenuity.</u>	<u>She can take charge with confidence.</u>
16. <u>Holding back emotions; fear of love.</u>	<u>No help from the environment.</u>	

WHAT DO I EXPECT?

Cards: P1 <u>The Hierophant</u> P2 <u>Ten of Swords</u>
     (Major Arcana V)

Worksheet #1 (cont.)

Meanings	**Stances**	**Heartlink**
17. Hearing; inner teacher; organized religion.	She knows she can count on her faith and inner wisdom.	He leans on her.
18. Release from obsession; viewpoints being transformed.	He expects their growth to free him from old attitudes.	

WHERE DOES ALL THIS LEAD?

Cards: P1 Queen of Cups   P2 Eight of Wands

Meanings	**Stances**	**Heartlink**
19. Sensitive; imaginative; emotionally responsive.	Her sensitive responsiveness and involvement will be pivotal in shaping their interaction.	Not only does she respond with sensitivity as he grows and changes, but her response will guide and encourage him.
20. Up in the air; movement; growth.	He has a lot of ideas to try.	

WHAT ELSE IS NEW?

Cards: P1 The Fool (Major Arcana 0)   P2 Queen of Wands

Meanings	**Stances**	**Heartlink**
21. Adventure of life; choice without fear.	She has a new freedom of choice.	She will be able to be more adventurous in

Worksheet #1 (cont.)

Meanings	*Stances*	*Heartlink*
22. Successful; openness.	He experiences a new openness.	response to his openness and domesticity.

Insights   *Plan(s) of Action*

As this was a practice exercise, no clients were present to state insights or arrive at plans of action.

Worksheet #2

Heartstyles

Person 1 _Woman_   Person 2 _Man_

Question _How can my boyfriend and I make_   Date _____

better use of our time together?

Heartprints	*Heartlinks*	*Heartstyle*
Where am I?	He will support her ideas.	Now they are ready to work together.
Where have I been?	They have worked separately.	
		Current or long-standing viewpoints
	*	*
Where have I been?	They have worked separately.	His withdrawal alerted her to how little they have worked together.
What's been happening?	His withdrawal alerted and concerned her.	
		Possible changes affecting the interaction
	*	*
What's in my way?	If she is persistent, he will work through past conditioning.	Through her persistence and his work, they achieve balance and harmony in their relationship.
What's in store for me?	Both will experience harmony and balance in the relationship.	
		Effects of acceptance or rejection of challenge

Worksheet #2 (cont.)

Heartprints	*Heartlinks*	*Heartstyle*
Where am I?	He will support her ideas.	They will need to be vigilant of
Who do I think I am?	They both have attitudes that hold them back.	those negative attitudes.
		How outer behavior conforms to inner belief
	*	*
What are my options?	Both will be more satisfied in the relationship.	Her leadership results in success.
What do I expect?	He leans on her.	
		Are expectations realistic for unfolding potential?
	*	*

Worksheet #3

Power Patterns

Person 1 <u>Woman</u>   Person 2 <u>Man</u>

Question <u>How can my boyfriend and I make</u>   Date _____

<u>make better use of our time together?</u>

Tally			*Pattern Interpretation*

1. Major Arcana P-1 <u>3</u>   Both are somewhat introspective and will

P-2 <u>3</u>   have to struggle against their respective

habits to change the quality of their time

together.

2. Court Cards P-1 <u>1</u>   Not a lot of outside influence. This issue is

P-2 <u>1</u>   between them.

3. Suits

   Wands P-1 <u>1</u>   She is not being as creative as she might be

in contributing ideas and taking initiative.

P-2 <u>3</u>   He is ambitious and enterprising, and

needs to put more of that into the

relationship and to create some of the

ideas for how they can have higher-

quality time together.

   Cups P-1 <u>4</u>   She is more romantic and open than he is.

P-2 <u>1</u>   He definitely needs more of this, which is

what she has to offer to complement their

difference in "sword" approaches.

Worksheet #3 (cont.)

		Tally	**Pattern Interpretation**
Swords	P-1	2	They need more balance here, too. He is
	P-2	4	more oriented toward "survival." She
			needs to recognize his need for survival.
			Perhaps he can see her "easier" way of
			assertiveness. In teaching one
			another, they have the opportunity to
			change their perspectives.
Pentacles	P-1	1	Both will need to stretch to bring about a
	P-2	0	change in their relationship, to accomplish
			flexibility in their thinking about it, and to
			include more practical considerations.
4. Duplicate	P-1	___	
Numbers	P-2	2-9s	He shows a tendency toward selflessness
			and giving.
5. Duplicate	P-1	1	9/Swords. They are comparable in having
Cards	P-2	1	the inner abilities necessary to affect
			decision making and to examine illusions.

BIBLIOGRAPHY

Anonymous, *Keystone of Tarot Symbols*. San Francisco, Epiphany Press, 1979.

Arrien, Angeles, *The Tarot Handbook*. Sonoma, Calif., Arcus Publishing, 1987.

Balin, Peter, *The Flight of Feathered Serpent*, 2d ed. Wilmot, Wis., Arcana Publishing Co., 1978.

Barrett, Clive, *The Norse Tarot*. Wellingborough, Northamptonshire, The Aquarian Press, 1989.

Bennett, Sidney, *Tarot for the Millions*. Los Angeles, Sherbourne Press, Inc., 1967.

Berne, Eric, *Games People Play*. New York, Grove Press, Inc., 1964.

Bridges, Carol, *Medicine Woman Tarot*. Stamford, Conn., U. S. Games Systems, Inc., 1989.

Campbell, Joseph, and Roberts, Richard, *Tarot Revelations*, 2d ed. San Anselmo, Calif., Vernal Equinox Press, 1982.

Cirlot, J. E., *A Dictionary of Symbols*, 2d ed. New York, Philosophical Library, 1971.

Condon, Thomas, *Expanded Intuition Training*. Workbook and six cassette tapes, Berkeley, Calif., The Changeworks, 1987.

Connolly, Eileen, *Tarot. A New Handbook for the Journeyman*. North Hollywood, Calif., Newcastle Publishing Co., Inc., 1979.

Cooper, J. C., *An Illustrated Encyclopedia of Traditional Symbols*. London, Thames and Hudson, 1978.

Culbert, Steven, *Reveal the Secrets of the Sacred Rose*. London and New York, W. Foulsham & Co., Ltd., 1988.

Curtiss, Harriette A. and F. H., *The Key to the Universe*, 6th rev. ed. North Hollywood, Calif., Newcastle Publishing Co., Inc., 1983.

Curtiss, Harriette A. and F. H., *The Key of Destiny*, 4th ed. North Hollywood, Calif., Newcastle Publishing Co., Inc., 1983.

Douglas, Nik, and Slinger, Penny, *The Secret Dakini Oracle*. New York, Destiny Books, 1979.

Emerson, Ralph W., *Selected Prose and Poetry*. San Francisco, Rinehart, 1969.

Ferguson, R. A., *Psychic Telemetry: New Key to Health, Wealth and Perfect Living*. West Nyack, N.Y., Parker Publishing Co., Inc., 1977.

Garen, Nancy, *Complete Tarot Workbook*. Westlake Village, Calif., Coltrane and Beach, 1984.

Gerulskis-Estes, Susan, *The Book of Tarot*. Dobbs Ferry, N.Y., Morgan & Morgan, 1981.

Golowin, Sergius, *The World of the Tarot*. York Beach, Maine, Samuel Weiser, Inc., 1988.

Graves, F. D., *The Windows of Tarot*. Dobbs Ferry, N.Y., Morgan & Morgan, 1973.

Gray, Eden, *Mastering the Tarot*. New York, Crown Publishers, 1971.

Gray, Eden, *The Tarot Revealed*. New York, New American Library, 1960.

Hall, James, *Dictionary of Subjects and Symbols in Art*. London, John Murray, 1974.

Hall, Manly P., "The Pythagorean Theory of Numbers." *PRS Journal, 24*, #1 (Summer 1964), pp. 22–33.

Hanson-Roberts, Mary, *Hanson-Roberts Tarot Deck*. New York, U. S. Games Systems, Inc., 1985.

Heline, Corinne, *The Bible and the Tarot*. Oceanside, Calif., New Age Press, Inc., 1969.

Hoeller, Stephan A., *The Royal Road*. Wheaton, Ill., The Theosophical Publishing House, 1975.

Hope, Murry, *Practical Techniques of Psychic Self-Defense*. New York, St. Martin's Press, 1983.

Houston, Jean, *Lifeforce: The Psycho-Historical Recovery of the Self*. New York, Dell Publishing Co., 1980.

Junjulas, Craig, *Psychic Tarot*. Dobbs Ferry, N.Y., Morgan & Morgan, 1985.

Kandinsky, Wassily, *Kandinsky: Complete Writings on Art,* Kenneth C. Lindsay and Peter Vergo, eds. London, Faber and Faber, 1982.

Kaplan, Stuart R., *The Encyclopedia of Tarot*, Vol. I. New York, U. S. Games Systems, Inc., 1978.

Kelen, Betty, *The Language of the Tarot*. N.p., Rota Press, 1974.

Konraad, Sandor, *Numerology. Key to the Tarot*. Rockport, Mass., Para Research, 1983.

Lammey, William C., *Karmic Tarot*. North Hollywood, Calif., Newcastle Publishing Co., Inc., 1988.

Laurence, Theodor, *The Sexual Key to the Tarot*. New York, The Citadel Press, 1971.

LeMieux, David, *Forbidden Images*. New York, Barnes & Noble Books, 1985.

Lotterhand, Jason C., *The Thursday Night Tarot*. North Hollywood, Calif., Newcastle Publishing Co., Inc., 1989.

Matthews, Caitlin and John, *The Arthurian Tarot*. Wellingborough, Northamptonshire, The Aquarian Press, 1990.

Mickaharic, Draja, *Spiritual Cleansing*. York Beach, Maine, Samuel Weiser, Inc., 1982.

Moore, Daphna, *The Rabbi's Tarot*. Lakewood, Colo., Hughes Henshaw Publications, 1987.

Newman, Kenneth D., *The Tarot. A Myth of Male Initiation*. New York, C. G. Jung Foundation for Analytical Psychology, 1983.

Neville, E. W., *Tarot for Lovers*. West Chester, Pa., Whitford Press, 1987.

Noble, Vicki, *Motherpeace: A Way to the Goddess through Myth, Art and Tarot*. San Francisco, Harper & Row, 1983.

O'Neill, Robert V., *Tarot Symbolism*. Lima, Ohio, Fairway Press, 1986.

Ouspensky, P.D., *The Symbolism of the Tarot*. New York, Dover Publications, Inc., 1976.

Peach, Emily, *The Tarot Workbook*. Wellingborough, Northamptonshire, The Aquarian Press, 1984.

Perls, Fritz S., *Gestalt Therapy Verbatim*. Moab, Utah, Real People Press, 1969.

Pollack, Rachel, *Salvador Dali's Tarot*. Salem, N.H., Salem House, 1985.

Pollack, Rachel, *Seventy-Eight Degrees of Wisdom. Part I: The Major Arcana*. Wellingborough, Northamptonshire, The Aquarian Press, 1980.

Pollack, Rachel, *Seventy-Eight Degrees of Wisdom. Part 2: The Minor Arcana and Readings*. Wellingborough, Northamptonshire, The Aquarian Press, 1983.

Pollack, Rachel, *Tarot: The Open Labyrinth*. Wellingborough, Northamptonshire, The Aquarian Press, 1986.

Quntanna, Beatrex, *Tarot: A Universal Language*. Carlsbad, Calif., Art Ala Carte Publishing, 1989.

Roark, Anne C., "Marriage Therapy. High Divorce Rates Lead Father of Cognitive Therapy to Write a Pop Book for Troubled Couples." *Los Angeles Times,* Part V, (Nov. 29, 1988) pp. 1, 3.

Robbins, Morgan, *Morgan's Tarot*. New York, U. S. Games Systems, Inc., 1983.

Saunders, E. Dale, *Mudra. A Study of Symbolic Gestures in Japanese Buddhist Sculpture*. Princeton, N.J., Princeton University Press, 1960.

Sharman-Burke, Juliet, *The Mythic Tarot Workbook*. New York, Simon & Schuster, Inc., 1988.

Steinbrecher, Edwin C., *The Inner Guide Meditation*. Santa Fe, N.M., Blue Feather Press, 1970.

Terranova, Jerry, *Names and Numbers: Doorways to Self-Discovery*. Unpublished manuscript, Los Angeles, 1985.

Thierens, A. E., *Astrology & the Tarot*. North Hollywood, Calif., Newcastle Publishing Co., Inc., 1975.

Waite, Arthur E., *The Pictorial Key to the Tarot*. Blauvelt, N.Y., Rudolf Steiner Publications, 1971.

Waite, Arthur E., *The Pictorial Key to the Tarot*. York Beach, Maine, Samuel Weiser, Inc., 1986.

Wang, Robert, *The Qabalistic Tarot*. York Beach, Maine, Samuel Weiser, Inc., 1983.

Wanless, James, *Voyager Tarot*. Carmel, Calif., Merrill-West Publishing, 1980.

Wasserman, James, *Instructions for Aleister Crowley's Tarot Deck*. New York, U. S. Games Systems, Inc., 1978.

Willis, Tony, *Magick and the Tarot*. Wellingborough, Northamptonshire, The Aquarian Press, 1988.

Index

ABOUT THE AUTHORS

Prior to his first trip to Egypt in 1984, **Robert E. Mueller,** Ph.D., became interested in the Tarot as a way of symbolically translating the experiences of the trip. He used the Tarot as a daily focus for growth on that trip, as well as on subsequent trips to Greece, Austria, France, and Bali, and a second trip to Egypt.

During a 1989 trip to London and southern England, Dr. Mueller, his wife, and his coauthor developed a Tarot ritual which they used for daily group focus as they visited sacred sites and power places. In June 1990 he traveled to Iceland to give Tarot readings and to visit sacred sites.

Dr. Mueller has studied with a number of teachers, including Eileen Connolly and James Wanless, creator of the Voyager Tarot deck.

He has created and taught workshops for beginning Tarot readers. He reads five different decks and owns an extensive Tarot deck collection.

Robert Mueller's doctorate is in human relations. Certified as a Master Postural Integrator, he has developed his own program of psychophysical body therapy, Release & Reorientation (R & R), which gently corrects postural imbalances that reflect and influence a person's attitudes toward life and relationships. He is a member of the American Massage Therapy Association and the California Massage Therapy Association, and a diplomate of the American Board of Sexology.

Signe E. Echols has a master's degree in education from the University of Southern California and was a teacher with the Los Angeles city schools for many years. A student of metaphysics for the past twenty-five years, she has studied the cabala and the Tarot with Dr. Stephan Hoeller, author of *The Royal Road.* She has also studied the use of the B.O.T.A. deck (designed by Paul Foster Case) with Builders of the Adytum.

An ordained minister of the Church of Inner Light in Los Angeles, the Reverend Signe Echols uses the Tarot in conjunction with the spiritual counseling offered after church services and in her own private practice. She is a member of the United Sensitives of America and reads with them at Whole Life Expos in Los Angeles, Pasadena, San Francisco, and San Diego.

Rev. Signe Echols has attended twice-weekly classes in ancient wisdom teachings and Jungian psychology since 1984 at the Philosophical Research Society in Los Angeles, founded by the late Manly P. Hall. She participates weekly in Roger Weir's spiritual personality development class, which she has been attending since 1987 at the Whirling Rainbow Institute, Los Angeles.

Her familiarity with the types of questions people bring to a Tarot session and her experience in teaching Tarot classes led her to realize the need for a relationship approach to readings.

Sandra A. Thomson is a free-lance writer specializing in travel, metaphysical topics, and features. Currently she is the chief financial officer on the board of IWOSC, Corp., the for-profit branch of IWOSC, Inc., Independent Writers of Southern California.